School Infrastructure in Paraguay

A WORLD BANK STUDY

School Infrastructure in Paraguay
Needs, Investments, and Costs

Quentin Wodon

© 2016 International Bank for Reconstruction and Development/The World Bank
1818 H Street NW, Washington DC 20433
Telephone: 202-473-1000; Internet: www.worldbank.org

Some rights reserved

1 2 3 4 19 18 17 16

World Bank Studies are published to communicate the results of the Bank's work to the development community with the least possible delay. The manuscript of this paper therefore has not been prepared in accordance with the procedures appropriate to formally edited texts.

This work is a product of the staff of The World Bank with external contributions. The findings, interpretations, and conclusions expressed in this work do not necessarily reflect the views of The World Bank, its Board of Executive Directors, or the governments they represent. The World Bank does not guarantee the accuracy of the data included in this work. The boundaries, colors, denominations, and other information shown on any map in this work do not imply any judgment on the part of The World Bank concerning the legal status of any territory or the endorsement or acceptance of such boundaries.

Nothing herein shall constitute or be considered to be a limitation upon or waiver of the privileges and immunities of The World Bank, all of which are specifically reserved.

Rights and Permissions

This work is available under the Creative Commons Attribution 3.0 IGO license (CC BY 3.0 IGO) http://creativecommons.org/licenses/by/3.0/igo. Under the Creative Commons Attribution license, you are free to copy, distribute, transmit, and adapt this work, including for commercial purposes, under the following conditions:

Attribution—Please cite the work as follows: Wodon, Quentin. 2016. *School Infrastructure in Paraguay: Needs, Investments, and Costs.* World Bank Studies. Washington, DC: World Bank. doi: 10.1596/978-1-4648-0448-9. License: Creative Commons Attribution CC BY 3.0 IGO

Translations—If you create a translation of this work, please add the following disclaimer along with the attribution: *This translation was not created by The World Bank and should not be considered an official World Bank translation. The World Bank shall not be liable for any content or error in this translation.*

Adaptations—If you create an adaptation of this work, please add the following disclaimer along with the attribution: *This is an adaptation of an original work by The World Bank. Views and opinions expressed in the adaptation are the sole responsibility of the author or authors of the adaptation and are not endorsed by The World Bank.*

Third-party content—The World Bank does not necessarily own each component of the content contained within the work. The World Bank therefore does not warrant that the use of any third-party-owned individual component or part contained in the work will not infringe on the rights of those third parties. The risk of claims resulting from such infringement rests solely with you. If you wish to re-use a component of the work, it is your responsibility to determine whether permission is needed for that re-use and to obtain permission from the copyright owner. Examples of components can include, but are not limited to, tables, figures, or images.

All queries on rights and licenses should be addressed to the Publishing and Knowledge Division, The World Bank, 1818 H Street NW, Washington, DC 20433, USA; fax: 202-522-2625; e-mail: pubrights@worldbank.org.

ISBN (paper): 978-1-4648-0448-9
ISBN (electronic): 978-1-4648-0449-6
DOI: 10.1596/978-1-4648-0448-9

Cover design: Debra Naylor, Naylor Design, Inc.

Library of Congress Cataloging-in-Publication Data has been requested

Contents

Acknowledgments ix
Abbreviations xi

Chapter 1	Introduction	1
	Organization	1
Chapter 2	Basic Infrastructure Diagnostic for Public Schools	5
	Abstract	5
	Introduction	5
	Brief Diagnostic of Paraguay's Education System	6
	State of Basic Infrastructure in Schools	8
	Index of Basic School Infrastructure Quality	13
	Conclusion	19
Chapter 3	Budget Allocations and Funding Needs for School Infrastructure	21
	Abstract	21
	Introduction	21
	Budget Allocations for School Infrastructure	23
	Decomposition of Budget Shares for Basic School Infrastructure	25
	Funding Needs for School Infrastructure	29
	Conclusion	34
Chapter 4	Primary School Infrastructure and Student Performance	35
	Abstract	35
	Introduction	35
	Methodology and Summary Statistics	37
	Regression Estimates	42
	Conclusion	45

Chapter 5	Classroom Gaps and Targeting Performance of Investments	47
	Abstract	47
	Introduction	47
	Methodology and Data	48
	Results	52
	Conclusion	55
	Notes	55

Bibliography 57

Figures

3.1	Budget for Investment and Construction and Equipment, 2012 PYG	23
3.2	Budget for Construction and Equipment in Basic and Upper Secondary Education, 2012 PYG	24
3.3	Budget Shares for Construction and Equipment	24

Tables

2.1	Summary of PREAL's Diagnostic of Paraguay's Education System	7
2.2	Public Education Spending and Spending Per Student, 1999 and 2010	8
2.3	Functioning Basic School Infrastructure by Area and by Education Level	10
2.4	Facilities in Need of Repairs as Share of Facilities in Good or Average Condition by Area and by Education Level	12
2.5	Facilities in Construction as Share of Facilities Being Used by Area and by Education Level	13
2.6	Factorial Analysis of Basic School Infrastructure	14
2.7	Index of Basic School Infrastructure by Department	15
2.8	Location Correlates for the Logarithm of the Normalized Index of Basic School Infrastructure Quality	18
3.1	Budgets and Budget Shares Allocated to Basic School Infrastructure Investments	26
3.2	Decomposition of Average Rates of Year-on-year Changes in Budget Shares	28
3.3	Estimation of the Potential Budgetary Cost of Selected Basic Amenities for Paraguay's Schools	30
3.4	Potential Budgetary Cost of New Classrooms for Paraguay's Schools	33
4.1	Impact on Test Scores of School Infrastructure and Pedagogical Supplies	38

4.2	Summary Statistics for the Variables of Interest, Paraguay 2008 (Not Weighted)	40
4.3	Correlates of Primary Public School Passing Rates, Paraguay 2008	43
5.1	School Infrastructure Poverty and Inequality Measures ($n=30$)	52
5.2	Analysis of the Targeting Performance of Classrooms in Construction ($n=30$)	53
5.3	Sensitivity Analysis of Infrastructure Poverty Measures to the Norms Used	54
5.4	Sensitivity Analysis of Targeting Performance Indicators to the Norms Used	54
5.5	Benefit Incidence Analysis of New Classrooms and Classrooms Not in Use	55

Acknowledgments

This study was written at the World Bank as an input for a nonlending technical assistance task for Paraguay managed by Rafael de Hoyos in the Latin America Region and as part of a work program on education costing managed by Quentin Wodon in the Education Global Practice. Partial funding for the study was provided by a grant from the Global Partnership Education for work on out-of-school children and education costing. Comments and suggestions from Rafael de Hoyos and Jessica Rodriguez are also gratefully acknowledged. The opinions expressed in this study are only those of the author and need not represent those of the World Bank, its Executive Directors, or the countries they represent.

Abbreviations

CAI	Classroom Availability Index
CO_2	carbon dioxide
C&E	construction and equipment
GDP	gross domestic product
MEC	Ministry of Education and Culture
NI	Normalized School Infrastucture Index
PPP	purchasing power parity
PREAL	*Progreso Educativo del Programa de Promoción de la Reforma Educativa en América Latina y el Caribe*
PYG	Paraguay guaraní

CHAPTER 1

Introduction

Organization

What is the state of school infrastructure for primary and secondary education in Paraguay? How much is invested by the government in order to improve school infrastructure and how have these investments evolved over time? What is the legal framework for such investments and is it appropriate? Given budget constraints, which types of investments are likely to be most needed in order to help improve student learning? Finally, how well targeted to the schools most in need are the infrastructure investments being made today? In order to help inform decision making by the Ministry of Education in this area, the objective of this study is to provide tentative answers to those questions on the basis of administrative budget data as well as school-level data collected through a 2008 school infrastructure census.

The literature on education production functions suggests that better basic infrastructure in school is likely to have a positive impact on school attainment and learning. While this impact may not necessarily be very large, students should be able to learn in an adequate physical environment. At the same time, many countries including Paraguay face hard budget constraints. It is therefore important to assess not only how much investments are needed in schools but also which types of school infrastructure investments are likely to bring the most benefits, and in which schools new investments should be made. The purpose of this study is to provide a preliminary analysis of these issues using both administrative budget data and school-level data in order to help inform decision making by the Ministry of Education.

The study consists of four chapters apart from this introduction. Chapter 2 provides a basic diagnostic of the state of infrastructure in Paraguay's public primary and secondary schools. The analysis is based on data from a 2008 school infrastructure census. Paraguay's school infrastructure appears to be in relatively poor shape and less well developed than that of other Latin American countries. In general, areas with higher levels of unmet basic needs as well as rural areas have a lower aggregate index of school infrastructure quality and differences are also observed between departments. While none of these findings are surprising, they help set the stage for more detailed analysis in subsequent chapters.

Chapter 3 provides an analysis of trends in past budget allocations to basic primary and secondary school infrastructure. The analysis suggests that there has been a sharp reduction in such allocations in recent years. In addition, the chapter assesses the potential investments that would be needed in order to reduce the school infrastructure gaps in the country. Given that Paraguay has adopted standards for what schools should have as infrastructure amenities, the cost of fulfilling these requirements is first estimated. The resulting cost is found to be very high and beyond reach, given budget constraints. Alternative suggestions are made for prioritizing basic infrastructure investments, and the cost of these alternative rules is also estimated.

One of the conclusions of the chapter is that while standards have been adopted in Paraguay as in many other countries as to what schools should be equipped with, such standards are useful only to the extent that they are ambitious but also somewhat realistic. In Paraguay, the requirement that all primary and secondary schools be equipped with (among others) direction and secretarial rooms, as well as one classroom per grade, a room for recreation and physical education, a library, and a laboratory is too ambitious. The cost of providing these amenities would be much too high, especially in a context where budget allocations for school construction and equipment have been reduced. Rather than aiming to equip all schools with as many amenities as possible, a better approach—recognized in practice by the Ministry—is to allocate the most important amenities where they are the most needed, and to build from that.

Chapter 4 then considers the question of which amenities are most needed. There is some degree of consensus in the literature that better basic infrastructure in schools improves student learning. But not all infrastructure investments are likely to have the same impacts on student performance. On the basis of the estimation of an education production function, the evidence provided in chapter 4 suggests that in Paraguay investments in classrooms in those schools that do not have enough classrooms are likely to bring larger gains than other investments. Furthermore, the largest gains tend to be observed when investing in the schools that are the most crowded in terms of a lack of classrooms. These results were obtained with limited data and may suffer from (among others) omitted variable bias, but they seem to be robust as well as intuitive and thus provide a useful guide to policy makers for allocating scarce resources.

Finally, chapter 5 looks at whether investments in classrooms are well targeted. This assessment of course depends on what the criteria for good targeting are. The idea is that since crowding in classrooms has been identified in chapter 4 as detrimental for student performance, it would be logical to target investments to provide classrooms in areas where crowding is most severe. Using poverty measurement techniques, the chapter provides a simple framework for conducting this type of analysis. The analysis suggests that needs are large with most of the student population being in schools that do not have enough classrooms. But it also suggests that investments in new classroom construction do not seem to be targeted to the schools that need more classrooms the most. There is a difficult trade-off here. On the one hand, poorer areas lack many infrastructure amenities, and it may seem appropriate to provide more classrooms to (rural) schools that have few of them. But on the other hand, the available measures of crowding in classrooms are higher in some of the better-off (urban) areas. It does seem from the analysis that too many classroom investments are being made in rural areas that may not need classrooms as much as alternative forms of teaching to better serve the population (such as multigrade teaching). While more analysis would be needed to look at the policy implications of this trade-off, the analysis provided in chapter 5 suggests that classroom investments do not reach the areas where crowding in classrooms is highest, and this is a source of concern that merits further attention. Finally, the analysis suggests that there may also be some potential in using classrooms currently not in use in order to reduce the lack of classrooms faced by many schools.

CHAPTER 2

Basic Infrastructure Diagnostic for Public Schools

Abstract

There is some consensus in the education literature that better basic infrastructure in schools improves student learning. The literature on education production functions suggests that a lack of basic amenities in schools inputs may affect student learning negatively. This study explores various questions related to basic school infrastructure needs, costs, and investments in Paraguay. As a start, this chapter provides a basic diagnostic of the state of infrastructure in public primary and secondary schools using data from a 2008 school census. The findings suggest that while some schools have the infrastructure amenities they need, many do not, especially in rural and poorer areas.

Introduction

A recent review of the literature on education production functions completed by Glewwe et al. (2013) suggests that the availability of basic furniture (desks, tables, and chairs), electricity, school libraries, and high-quality walls, roofs, and floors in schools all may have positive impacts on learning. In the case of Paraguay, research by Otter and Villalobos Barría (2009) also suggests that schools with better infrastructure perform better, which is not too surprising.

In order to ensure proper basic infrastructure in schools, Paraguay has adopted (like many other countries) standards for its schools. In its 1999 Decree 6589 and through Resolution 3985, the Ministry of Education and Culture (MEC) stipulated that all schools should have (i) a direction room; (ii) a secretarial room; (iii) at least one classroom (7.2 meter × 7.2 meter) per grade with proper ventilation and light; (iv) separate bathrooms for boys and girls; (v) a proper space for recreation and physical education; (vi) drinking water; and (vii) a library. In addition, each school should also have a laboratory for teaching physics, chemistry, and the natural sciences (Rivarola and Elías 2013). Unfortunately, despite such provisions, in comparison to other Latin American countries

Paraguay remains today one of the countries with the largest school infrastructure deficits (Duarte, Gargiulo, and Moreno 2011; Murillo and Román 2011).

The objective of this study is to explore various questions related to basic school infrastructure needs, costs, and investments in Paraguay. At the start of the study, it is useful to first provide a basic diagnostic of the state of infrastructure in public primary and secondary schools. This is the purpose of this chapter. The analysis is based on data from a 2008 school infrastructure census. The findings suggest that while some schools have the infrastructure amenities they need, many do not, especially in rural and poorer areas. This information and the school infrastructure census dataset are used in subsequent chapters for more detailed work on investments costs and needs and on the targeting of new investments, among others.

The structure of the chapter is as follows. First, in order to provide contextual information for the study, a brief diagnostic of Paraguay's education system is provided by summarizing a study recently completed by Elías, Molinas, and Misiego (2013). Next, the data from Paraguay's 2008 school infrastructure census are used to assess the share of schools and the share of the student population in schools with various amenities or facilities, as well as the share of facilities that are in poor condition and the level of investments under way at the time of the census. The next section then provides aggregate measures of school infrastructure quality to compare various areas and departments in the country. A brief conclusion follows.

Brief Diagnostic of Paraguay's Education System

In order to provide contextual information for the analysis carried in this chapter and the rest of this study, it is useful to provide a brief diagnostic of Paraguay's education system. Such a diagnostic was recently conducted by Elías, Molinas, and Misiego (2013) as part of the PREAL (*Progreso Educativo del Programa de Promoción de la Reforma Educativa en América Latina y el Caribe*) program. Table 2.1 provides the main conclusions of this diagnostic along nine areas of focus: coverage of the education system, retention in school, learning, equity, teacher profession, public investments in education, competencies and standards, monitoring and evaluation system, and finally autonomy and accountability. For each of those dimensions, a letter grade is provided, with the possible grades being Excellent; Good; Average; Insufficient; Poor. In addition, an assessment of changes in performance over time in each of the nine areas is provided with three potential notes: improvements, no change in performance, and deterioration.

Overall, the performance of Paraguay's education system is relatively weak and while there have been improvements in recent years for coverage, retention, and equity, there has been no change in all other dimensions with the exception of public investments in education, where there has been a decline in performance due to a reduction in public spending budgets for education as a share of

Table 2.1 Summary of PREAL's Diagnostic of Paraguay's Education System

Area	Grade	Trend
Coverage	Good	Improvement
Retention in school	Average	Improvement
Learning	Insufficient	No change
Equity	Insufficient	Improvement
Teacher profession	Insufficient	No change
Investments	Insufficient	Deterioration
Competencies and standards	Insufficient	No change
Monitoring and evaluation system	Average	No change
Autonomy and accountability	Average	No change

Source: Elías, Molinas, and Misiego 2013.
Note: Grading system: Excellent; Good; Average; Insufficient; Very poor.

gross domestic product (GDP) while other countries increased their investments in education.

Looking at each of the nine areas of focus one by one, the system is rated as good in terms of its coverage, essentially because the number of students enrolled has increased at all levels, with nearly universal rates of enrollment in primary schools. However, there has been a reduction in net primary school enrollment rates in the last few years, and a substantial share of children aged 13 to 17 are not in school, resulting in a lower rate of enrollment in Paraguay than in much of the rest of the region at the secondary level. Retention in school is rated as average, but with an improvement in the number of years of schooling of the adult population (15 years and above) from 7.1 years in 2000 to 8.2 years in 2010. Learning, however, is rated as insufficient on the basis of data from national assessments suggesting that more than half of students in third grade do not reach the expected level of proficiency in mathematics, and 40 percent do not reach the expected level of proficiency in Spanish. In a regional assessment of learning, Paraguay was in the bottom five countries. In terms of equity, there has been a reduction over time in the enrollment gap between urban and rural areas and between income groups. However, inequalities in education persist and are quite substantial, so that equity is rated as insufficient. Indigenous populations in particular still lag behind the national average.

Data on teachers are limited, but the available evidence suggests that the quality of teachers remains insufficient, with a lack of incentive for performance as well (teacher salaries are only minimally related to performance). Public spending for education as a share of GDP decreased from 5.1 percent in 1999 to 4.1 percent in 2010, at a time when other countries such as Argentina, Brazil, and Chile increased their investments in education (see table 2.2). Paraguay's investment primary and secondary per students in 2010 was one fourth to one fifth the level of investment of the other Latin American coun-

Table 2.2 Public Education Spending and Spending Per Student, 1999 and 2010

	Argentina		Brazil		Chile		Paraguay	
	1999	2010	1999	2010	1999	2010	1999	2010
Public education spending as share of GDP (%)	4.6	6.2	4.0	5.8	4.0	4.9	5.1	4.1
Spending per primary school student (2009 PPP $)	1,416	2,373	859	2,026	3,405	2,360	541	475
Spending per secondary school student (2009 PPP $)	1,903	3,815	779	2,063	1,593	2,404	730	695

Source: Rivarola and Elías (2013) based on UNESCO and Ministry of Education data.
Note: GDP = gross domestic product; PPP = purchasing power parity.

tries listed in table 2.2. Paraguay is rated as insufficient in this area, and this is also the only area where there has been deterioration over time. As discussed in detail in subsequent sections, this deterioration has also affected allocations to basic school infrastructure, which are now especially low and have been decreasing. As noted by Elías, Molinas, and Misiego (2013), when public spending may not be enough to cover teacher salaries and administrative costs, there is very little room available for investments.

The last three dimensions in table 2.1 relate to competencies and standards, monitoring and evaluation, and autonomy and accountability. The rating for competencies and standards is insufficient because despite efforts in that area, memorization still prevails in the classroom, as opposed to discovery, with little change over time. The other two dimensions—monitoring and evaluation, and autonomy and accountability—are both rated average without change over time. National assessment systems do exist, but are not always comparable, and while decentralization towards departments is on the book, it has not necessarily made a substantial difference, and more could be done to promote the participation of parent associations in school management.

State of Basic Infrastructure in Schools

A key finding from the brief diagnostic of Paraguay's education system presented in the previous section is the fact that public spending for education appears to be on the low side, both in percentage of GDP and in actual amounts spent per child. As discussed in more details in chapter 3, it can also be shown that the share of public education spending allocated to school construction and equipment has decreased dramatically over the last decade. The resources available to upgrade basic school infrastructure are thus very limited, while the needs are large.

One of the consequences of the lack of resources allocated to basic school infrastructure is that many schools are not well equipped today and do not meet the requirements of the Ministry's Decree 6589 and Resolution 3985 mentioned in the introduction to this chapter. Whether all of these requirements should be met is open to question, given their budgetary costs, and this will be discussed in the next chapter. But the fact that some schools lack basic infrastructure and important amenities is not in question. In this context, the objective of this section is to provide a review of the state of basic infrastructure in public school on the basis of the school infrastructure census implemented in 2008 by the Ministry of Education and Culture.

Table 2.3 provides summary statistics on the average number of classrooms and students per school, on a summary index of classroom adequacy to serve a school's student population, and on whether schools have a number of other amenities. The summary statistics are provided for the country as a whole (all schools), as well as separately for urban and rural areas, and for primary and secondary schools (if a school caters to both primary and secondary students, it will be included in both categories). Statistics are provided without weights, in which case each school counts for the same whatever its size, as well as weighted by the number of students in the school, in which case the statistics provide the share of students that benefit from a specific infrastructure (when computing weighted statistics for primary and secondary schools, if a school covers both cycles, only the number of students in primary or secondary grades is used for the weighting, so that the statistics represent the primary and secondary student population).

The average size of the schools is relatively large, especially in urban areas where the average school has 411 students. The figure for rural schools is 99 students. Secondary schools are larger (260 students on average) than primary schools (161 students). On average, schools have six classrooms in use—the figure is 10.6 classrooms in urban areas versus 4.7 classrooms in rural areas and 5.9 classrooms for primary schools versus 8.2 for secondary schools.

In order to assess the extent to which enough classrooms are available for the student population in each school, a classroom availability index is estimated. Denote this index by CAI_i. It represents the number of classrooms available in a school normalized by the number of classrooms that should be available so that a value of 100 means that the school has exactly the number of classrooms it needs, given its student population (all schools with an index value at or above 100 are not infrastructure poor). What does the term "should" mean? If one considers a benchmark baseline case in which one classroom should be available per set of $n = 30$ students in a school (other benchmarks such as $n = 20$, $n = 25$, or $n = 35$ could be considered, and this will be done in subsequent chapters), and if one denotes by CU_i the number of classrooms actually in use in a school (this information is available in the 2008 school infrastructure census) and by P_i and S_i the number of primary and secondary students, then the index CAI_i is defined as follows:

Table 2.3 Functioning Basic School Infrastructure by Area and by Education Level

	Schools (not weighted)					Students (schools weighted by number of students)				
	All schools	Urban	Rural	Primary	Secondary	All schools	Urban	Rural	Primary	Secondary
	Average values across schools									
Students and classrooms per school										
Number of students	167.5	411.2	99.3	160.8	260.5	n.a.	n.a.	n.a.	n.a.	n.a.
Number of classrooms being used	6.0	10.6	4.7	5.9	8.2	n.a.	n.a.	n.a.	n.a.	n.a.
	Share of schools or students with a characteristic or amenity (%)									
Share of schools by classroom index										
$0.75 \leq$ CAI	12.3	36.9	5.5	11.2	19.8	38.1	58.8	14.2	31.7	48.1
$0.75 <$ CAI ≤ 1.00	12.4	23.7	9.2	11.8	18.5	19.8	22.3	16.8	19.8	19.7
$1.00 <$ CAI ≤ 1.25	13.3	15.5	12.7	13.1	17.1	13.9	10.0	18.3	14.7	12.7
$1.25 <$ CAI ≤ 1.50	12.4	8.8	13.4	12.7	13.2	9.6	4.4	15.6	11.1	7.2
$1.50 <$ CAI ≤ 1.75	11.2	6.0	12.6	11.2	10.0	6.6	2.3	11.5	7.6	5.0
$1.75 <$ CAI	38.5	9.1	46.7	39.9	21.4	12.1	2.1	23.6	15.2	7.2
Share of schools with functioning amenities										
Toilets	61.6	95.2	52.2	59.7	76.8	84.2	98.5	67.7	80.1	90.5
Direction room	43.5	75.9	34.5	40.5	59.2	68.0	84.5	48.8	61.1	78.6
Secretarial room	12.1	36.0	5.4	8.9	20.7	33.7	53.8	10.4	23.1	49.9
Library	13.8	40.3	6.4	11.6	21.8	36.1	56.6	12.4	27.7	49.1
Laboratory	3.2	12.1	0.7	1.6	5.9	12.6	22.2	1.4	5.3	23.7
Workshop room	2.3	8.0	0.7	1.4	4.0	8.0	13.9	1.1	3.5	14.9
Multiuse room	3.8	11.1	1.8	2.8	5.7	10.4	17.3	2.4	6.1	17.1
Teachers' room	5.7	19.2	2.0	3.7	9.9	18.2	30.4	4.0	10.2	30.5
Recreation area	3.6	11.8	1.3	2.9	5.9	12.9	22.2	2.0	8.5	19.6
Sanitation/toilets	56.4	80.0	49.8	55.1	66.8	74.2	86.3	60.3	70.2	80.4
Electricity	92.5	99.5	90.6	92.0	98.1	98.1	99.9	96.0	97.2	99.5
Piped water	43.6	67.3	37.0	41.3	53.1	57.2	65.9	47.1	53.2	63.4
Computers	23.3	48.8	16.2	20.8	34.6	43.2	58.6	25.3	36.8	53.0
Access to the Internet	4.0	14.5	1.0	3.0	6.9	13.6	23.4	2.2	9.0	20.6
Number of schools	6,608	1,445	5,163	5,192	3,520	6,608	1,445	5,163	5,192	3,520

Source: Computations from Paraguay's 2008 school infrastructure census.
Note: n.a. = not applicable.

$$CAI_i = \frac{CU_i \times n \times 100}{P_i + S_i} \quad \text{with} \quad n = 30 \tag{2.1}$$

Again, the value of n can be changed, and this will be done in subsequent chapters when discussing budgetary costs (in chapter 3) and infrastructure gaps (in chapter 5), but for the basic statistics provided in this chapter, a value of $n = 30$ will simply be used. Apart from some reasonable norm in terms of classroom availability that should be based on a school's student population, it is important to note that as mentioned in the introduction, Paraguay has a separate norm that requires in principle all schools to have at least one classroom per grade (thus primary schools with six grades would need in principle at least six classrooms; this is clearly not the case, since the average number of classrooms in all primary schools taken together is 5.9, with many schools having much fewer classrooms than the implicit norm of six classrooms). One could challenge this rule, since at least in small rural primary schools the cost of implementing the rule is likely to be much higher than relying on multigrade teaching. Therefore, rather than reporting the number of schools or the share of students in schools with less than six classrooms, for the purpose of this chapter statistics on the classroom availability index are reported.

Table 2.3 suggests that 12.3 percent of the schools have a classroom availability index below 0.75. When weighting the schools by their student population, this rises to 38.1 percent, suggesting that in many schools, classrooms may be crowded (increasing the parameter n for the estimation would reduce these shares, while reducing the parameter would increase the shares). Importantly, using the classroom availability index, schools appear to be more crowded in urban than in rural areas, and in secondary than primary schools. This is in part because many rural schools are small, so that even if a classroom is not available for each grade, the index does not suggest a lack of classroom to accommodate the student population.

The next part of the table provides data on the share of schools with various basic amenities. Among all schools, 92.5 percent have electricity, 61.6 percent have independent toilets, and 56.4 have sanitation (which also includes toilets), but for all other amenities, less than half of the schools are equipped with those amenities. Specifically, 43.5 percent of the schools have a direction room, 43.6 percent have piped water, 23.3 percent have computers, 13.8 percent have a library, 12.1 percent have a secretarial room, 5.7 percent have a teachers' room, and less than 5 percent have a workshop room, a multiuse room, a recreation area, and access to the Internet. Amenities are more common in urban areas and among secondary schools as expected, and similarly the share of students in schools with various amenities is higher, since larger schools tend to have more amenities.

Table 2.4 provides information on the share of facilities in need of repairs (computed as a share of the facilities in good or average condition). The shares are computed for each school, and then the average shares for all schools are displayed. It appears that with the exception of classrooms and sanitation, most of the facilities are in relatively good condition, since in table 2.2 the average shares across all schools of facilities in need of repairs tend to be below 5 percent. But in the case of sanitation, for an average school, the likelihood that the facilities are in poor condition is one fifth (20.1 percent), and the likelihood that a classroom will be in poor condition is above one tenth (11.1 percent for classrooms). Note that in those estimations, schools of different sizes are weighted equally. The fact that when looking at the student population the shares are lower suggests again that school infrastructure is better in larger schools.

Table 2.5 provides information on the share of facilities in construction (computed as a share of the facilities in use). Not surprisingly, given the fact that sanitation facilities and classrooms tend to be in poorer condition, much of the construction under way at the time of the school infrastructure census focused on classrooms and sanitation facilities. For classrooms, for an average school, construction would increase the availability of classrooms by 3.1 percentage points versus the number of classrooms in use, and for sanitation, the estimate is 2.3 percent. Of course, these are averages, and construction is concentrated in a relatively small number of schools. Of the 6,608 schools in the census, 592

Table 2.4 Facilities in Need of Repairs as Share of Facilities in Good or Average Condition by Area and by Education Level
percent

	Schools (not weighted)					Students (schools weighted by number of students)				
	All schools	Urban	Rural	Primary	Secondary	All schools	Urban	Rural	Primary	Secondary
Classrooms	11.1	3.5	13.2	11.9	7.7	6.2	2.6	10.3	7.7	3.8
Direction room	5.1	1.5	6.9	5.7	4.3	2.8	1.1	5.6	3.5	1.8
Secretarial room	1.2	0.8	1.7	1.4	0.9	0.6	0.5	1.2	0.9	0.4
Library	1.9	1.6	2.6	2.4	1.9	1.4	1.2	2.3	2.0	0.9
Laboratory	1.6	1.5	2.2	1.9	1.7	1.0	0.9	1.3	0.7	1.1
Workshop room	3.9	3.4	5.1	5.3	2.7	1.7	1.5	3.6	4.3	0.6
Multiuse room	3.1	2.7	3.6	4.5	1.3	2.0	2.0	1.7	4.3	0.7
Teachers' room	2.4	2.0	3.4	3.1	2.1	1.7	1.7	1.9	2.9	1.0
Recreation area	1.5	0.0	4.8	1.0	1.7	0.3	0.0	3.6	0.2	0.4
Sanitation	20.1	7.4	23.6	20.9	15.7	12.0	5.7	19.3	13.9	9.1

Source: Author's estimations from Paraguay's 2008 school infrastructure census.

Table 2.5 Facilities in Construction as Share of Facilities Being Used by Area and by Education Level
percent

	Schools (not weighted)					Students (schools weighted by number of students)				
	All schools	Urban	Rural	Primary	Secondary	All schools	Urban	Rural	Primary	Secondary
Classrooms	3.1	2.8	3.1	3.0	3.4	2.9	2.4	3.5	3.0	2.9
Direction room	0.4	0.4	0.4	0.4	0.5	0.6	0.5	0.8	0.6	0.6
Secretarial room	0.2	0.1	0.3	0.3	0.2	0.3	0.2	1.2	0.5	0.2
Library	0.7	0.9	0.3	0.5	0.8	0.7	0.7	0.1	0.4	0.8
Laboratory	0.0	0.0	0.0	0.0	0.0	0.0	0.0	0.0	0.0	0.0
Workshop room	0.0	0.0	0.0	0.0	0.0	0.0	0.0	0.0	0.0	0.0
Multiuse room	0.0	0.0	0.0	0.0	0.0	0.0	0.0	0.0	0.0	0.0
Teachers' room	0.2	0.3	0.0	0.4	0.3	0.4	0.4	0.0	0.5	0.3
Recreation area	0.0	0.0	0.0	0.0	0.0	0.0	0.0	0.0	0.0	0.0
Sanitation	2.3	2.9	2.2	2.1	2.6	1.8	1.2	2.5	1.8	1.8

Source: Author's estimations from Paraguay's 2008 school infrastructure census.

schools have at least one classroom in construction (among those, 369 have exactly one additional classroom being built, while the other schools are building two or more classrooms), and 129 have sanitation and toilet facilities under construction. This priority given to classrooms and sanitation and toilets remains valid today, since in its 2013 micro-planning, the Ministry of Education and Culture identified as priorities the need to build or repair classrooms as well as sanitation/toilet facilities.

Overall, the conclusion from this brief diagnostic of the quality of basic school infrastructure in Paraguay is that many schools are missing amenities that clearly should be available, not only in terms of classrooms but also in terms of sanitation and toilets and libraries, among others. While some of the other amenities could be considered as optional, the share of the schools benefitting from such amenities remains low even among secondary schools.

Index of Basic School Infrastructure Quality

It is also useful to construct an aggregate index of basic school infrastructure, but when doing so the question of the weights to be assigned to different school characteristics or amenities needs to be considered. One possibility would be to assign equal weight to different amenities, but this is not likely to reflect well overall differences in infrastructure quality between schools. Ideally, one might want to assign weights for each infrastructure characteristics on the basis of the role that different amenities play in student learning, but as discussed in chapter 4, it is not clear that some of the amenities actually have an impact on learning. The alternative used here is to let the weights be determined by the data through a factorial analysis, whereby weights are defined in such a way that the initial variance in the data is explained as much as possible by different factors. The first such factor provided by the factorial analysis then represents—at least in first approximation—an overall index of school infrastructure quality. The list of variables used for the factorial analysis is provided in table 2.6 together with the weights assigned to each variable. Note that because factorial analysis aims to generate factors that account for the largest possible share of the variance observed in the initial variables, some variables may be weighted relatively low, but this does not necessarily mean that they do not matter. For example, probably in part because most schools have electricity, this variable does not factor heavily in the overall index of infrastructure quality, but this does not mean that electricity does not matter. What the index does provide is a measure of differences between schools in amenities, with the measure defined implicitly to differentiate schools.

If one denotes the index obtained from the factorial analysis by I_i, a normalized index taking values between zero and 100 can also be defined by using the following formula:

$$NI_i = \frac{I_i - \min(I_i)}{\max(I_i) - \min(I_i)} \quad (2.2)$$

Table 2.6 Factorial Analysis of Basic School Infrastructure

Amenities	Weight
Number of classrooms in use	0.215
Availability of:	
Direction room	0.137
Secretarial room	0.165
Library	0.156
Laboratory	0.126
Workshop room	0.085
Multiuse room	0.085
Teachers' room	0.139
Recreation area	0.077
Sanitation	0.083
Electricity	0.040
Piped water	0.049
Computers	0.100
Internet	0.095

Source: Author's estimations from Paraguay's 2008 school infrastructure census.

The advantage of the normalized index is that it facilitates the interpretation since a value of 100 is the best a school can achieve, while a value of zero is the lowest feasible rating. Table 2.7 provides measures by department of the normalized index of infrastructure quality, for all schools as well as for primary and secondary schools and for urban and rural areas separately. For example, when all schools are considered, the highest mean value for the index is observed not surprisingly for the Capital department. In the Capital city, schools on average have 43 percent of the maximum value for the index. At the other extreme, the department where schools on average have the lowest normalized infrastructure index is Caazapa (index value of 0.095), where schools on average have less than 10 percent of the amenities encountered in the best school in the country. Several departments (Canindeyu, San Pedro, Concepción, Presidente Hayes, Amambay, Caaguazu) do not fare much better, with values of the index below 0.120.

Table 2.7 Index of Basic School Infrastructure by Department

Variable	Number of schools	Mean index	Standard deviation	Minimum value	Maximum value
		All schools			
Alto Paraguay	29	0.152	0.128	0.013	0.449
Alto Parana	616	0.142	0.129	0.007	1.000
Amambay	159	0.113	0.134	0.007	0.721
Boquerón	38	0.143	0.164	0.007	0.669
Caaguazu	785	0.117	0.098	0.007	0.879
Caazapa	408	0.095	0.082	0.000	0.741
Canindeyu	378	0.096	0.095	0.000	0.567
Capital	106	0.431	0.196	0.062	0.887
Central	588	0.238	0.161	0.020	0.933
Concepción	359	0.104	0.111	0.000	0.936
Cordillera	329	0.174	0.125	0.035	0.769
Guaira	341	0.122	0.121	0.007	0.888
Itapua	731	0.123	0.113	0.007	0.927
Misiones	172	0.166	0.133	0.007	0.710
Paraguari	405	0.151	0.101	0.013	0.634
Presidente Hayes	156	0.106	0.132	0.000	0.682
San Pedro	838	0.103	0.080	0.000	0.721
Neembucu	170	0.134	0.117	0.007	0.896
		Primary schools			
Alto Paraguay	25	0.120	0.105	0.013	0.435
Alto Parana	571	0.134	0.120	0.007	1.000
Amambay	146	0.098	0.117	0.007	0.529

table continues next page

Table 2.7 Index of Basic School Infrastructure by Department *(continued)*

Variable	Number of schools	Mean index	Standard deviation	Minimum value	Maximum value
Boquerón	34	0.131	0.166	0.007	0.669
Caaguazu	699	0.107	0.083	0.007	0.616
Caazapa	355	0.086	0.071	0.007	0.741
Canindeyu	345	0.085	0.078	0.000	0.562
Capital	79	0.370	0.164	0.062	0.773
Central	524	0.226	0.147	0.020	0.867
Concepción	334	0.098	0.099	0.000	0.936
Cordillera	281	0.156	0.102	0.035	0.704
Guaira	292	0.109	0.101	0.007	0.888
Itapua	664	0.111	0.099	0.007	0.927
Misiones	154	0.147	0.109	0.007	0.629
Paraguari	371	0.140	0.086	0.013	0.634
Presidente Hayes	146	0.094	0.118	0.000	0.651
San Pedro	751	0.095	0.068	0.000	0.721
Neembucu	141	0.115	0.108	0.007	0.896
Secondary schools					
Alto Paraguay	13	0.195	0.156	0.013	0.449
Alto Parana	318	0.206	0.146	0.020	1.000
Amambay	46	0.239	0.161	0.037	0.721
Boquerón	15	0.267	0.197	0.037	0.669
Caaguazu	427	0.149	0.111	0.013	0.879
Caazapa	209	0.124	0.097	0.000	0.741
Canindeyu	206	0.130	0.108	0.007	0.567
Capital	97	0.441	0.201	0.062	0.887
Central	505	0.259	0.162	0.041	0.933
Concepción	178	0.156	0.135	0.013	0.936
Cordillera	173	0.226	0.142	0.048	0.769
Guaira	161	0.168	0.148	0.030	0.888
Itapua	293	0.188	0.136	0.035	0.927
Misiones	85	0.247	0.144	0.069	0.710
Paraguari	209	0.199	0.108	0.037	0.634
Presidente Hayes	74	0.173	0.160	0.035	0.682
San Pedro	465	0.131	0.093	0.020	0.721
Neembucu	46	0.234	0.155	0.041	0.896
Urban schools					
Alto Paraguay	7	0.229	0.081	0.137	0.357
Alto Parana	194	0.246	0.163	0.042	1.000
Amambay	41	0.255	0.163	0.007	0.721

table continues next page

Table 2.7 Index of Basic School Infrastructure by Department *(continued)*

Variable	Number of schools	Mean index	Standard deviation	Minimum value	Maximum value
Boquerón	2	0.583	0.122	0.497	0.669
Caaguazu	115	0.230	0.158	0.013	0.879
Caazapa	31	0.232	0.154	0.062	0.741
Canindeyu	37	0.255	0.128	0.069	0.546
Capital	106	0.431	0.196	0.062	0.887
Central	429	0.263	0.172	0.021	0.933
Concepción	38	0.269	0.206	0.027	0.936
Cordillera	61	0.325	0.171	0.075	0.769
Guaira	58	0.274	0.172	0.055	0.888
Itapua	91	0.292	0.179	0.035	0.927
Misiones	39	0.313	0.158	0.071	0.710
Paraguari	52	0.306	0.143	0.078	0.634
Presidente Hayes	21	0.276	0.196	0.069	0.682
San Pedro	84	0.198	0.148	0.034	0.721
Neembucu	39	0.267	0.153	0.065	0.896
Rural schools					
Alto Paraguay	22	0.127	0.132	0.013	0.449
Alto Parana	422	0.094	0.070	0.007	0.459
Amambay	118	0.063	0.075	0.007	0.423
Boquerón	36	0.119	0.128	0.007	0.569
Caaguazu	670	0.097	0.067	0.007	0.508
Caazapa	377	0.083	0.061	0.000	0.419
Canindeyu	341	0.079	0.073	0.000	0.567
Capital	n.a.	n.a.	n.a.	n.a.	n.a.
Central	159	0.172	0.098	0.020	0.520
Concepción	321	0.085	0.072	0.000	0.568
Cordillera	268	0.140	0.080	0.035	0.503
Guaira	283	0.091	0.077	0.007	0.731
Itapua	640	0.099	0.073	0.007	0.615
Misiones	133	0.123	0.087	0.007	0.620
Paraguari	353	0.128	0.068	0.013	0.499
Presidente Hayes	135	0.079	0.096	0.000	0.637
San Pedro	754	0.092	0.060	0.000	0.618
Neembucu	131	0.094	0.064	0.007	0.352

Source: Author's estimations from Paraguay's 2008 school infrastructure census.
Note: n.a. = not applicable.

The index values for primary schools are as expected well below those for secondary schools, and the same is observed for the values in rural areas as compared to those observed in urban areas. Finally, in table 2.8, descriptive regressions for the geographical correlates of the logarithm of the normalized index of school infrastructure quality are provided. The objective is simply to measure the marginal impact on school infrastructure associated with location. The explanatory variables include whether a school is located in urban or rural areas, whether the school combines primary and secondary grades, whether the school is located in areas with high levels of unmet basic needs, and departmental dummy variables. The indicators of unmet basic needs in housing, access to education, and the ability of households to make a livelihood were computed at the subdepartmental level with the 2002 census. As for the departmental dummy variables, Capital is the reference category (the indicators of unmet basic needs were not available for Alto Paraguay, so the few schools in that department are not included).

The results suggest that being located in urban areas generates a gain in the index of basic school infrastructure of about 60 percent versus being located in rural areas. When a primary school is combined with a secondary school, this increases infrastructure quality among primary schools, while by contrast, when a secondary school is combined with a primary school, this reduces the index among secondary schools. There is a clear negative relationship between unmet basic needs at the subdepartmental level and lower levels of basic

Table 2.8 Location Correlates for the Logarithm of the Normalized Index of Basic School Infrastructure Quality

Variable	Coefficient	Std. Error	P>|t|	Coefficient	Std. Error	P>|t|	Coefficient	Std. Error	P>|t|
		All schools			Primary schools			Secondary schools	
Location and type of school									
Urban location	0.635	0.022	***	0.586	0.025	***	0.612	0.025	***
Combined primary and secondary school	0.687	0.016	***	0.668	0.017	***	−0.152	0.028	***
Unmet basic needs									
Unmet basic needs— housing quality	−0.008	0.001	***	−0.007	0.001	***	−0.009	0.001	***
Unmet basic needs—access to education	−0.012	0.002	***	−0.012	0.002	***	−0.007	0.002	**
Unmet basic needs— livelihoods	−0.003	0.002		−0.003	0.002		−0.004	0.003	*

table continues next page

Table 2.8 Location Correlates for the Logarithm of the Normalized Index of Basic School Infrastructure Quality *(continued)*

	Coefficient	Std. Error	P>|t|	Coefficient	Std. Error	P>|t|	Coefficient	Std. Error	P>|t|
Variable	All schools			Primary schools			Secondary schools		
Department (reference: Capital)									
Alto Parana	−0.246	0.063	***	−0.169	0.070	**	−0.227	0.068	***
Amambay	−0.449	0.091	***	−0.412	0.099	***	−0.112	0.116	
Caaguazu	−0.228	0.063	***	−0.159	0.070	**	−0.244	0.068	***
Caazapa	−0.329	0.070	***	−0.272	0.078	***	−0.342	0.078	***
Canindeyu	−0.362	0.074	***	−0.312	0.081	***	−0.255	0.082	**
Central	−0.318	0.058	***	−0.238	0.065	***	−0.260	0.059	***
Concepción	−0.361	0.072	***	−0.295	0.078	***	−0.219	0.083	**
Cordillera	0.086	0.063		0.158	0.071	**	0.033	0.068	
Guaira	−0.214	0.068	**	−0.128	0.076	*	−0.273	0.077	***
Itapua	−0.104	0.065		−0.055	0.072		−0.098	0.071	
Misiones	−0.032	0.070		0.020	0.077		0.031	0.077	
Paraguari	0.058	0.062		0.131	0.070	*	0.064	0.066	
Presidente Hayes	−0.216	0.112	**	−0.215	0.120	*	−0.021	0.113	
San Pedro	−0.224	0.064	***	−0.158	0.072	**	−0.230	0.070	***
Neembucu	0.004	0.073		0.080	0.084		−0.059	0.092	
Constant	2.663	0.061	***	2.608	0.069	***	3.430	0.067	***
R-squared	0.486			0.467			0.390		
Number of observations	6,464			5,779			3,467		

Source: Author's estimations from Paraguay's 2008 school infrastructure census.
Note: Estimation through linear regression with robust standard errors. Statistical level of significance is 1 percent for ***, 5 percent for **, and 10 percent for *.

school infrastructure, especially for the indices of unmet basic needs related to housing and education. In addition, after accounting for such subdepartmental effects, many departments still fare worse than the reference department Capital. While these regressions are purely descriptive, they help in assessing the average magnitude of the marginal average gains or losses in the normalized basic infrastructure index associated with specific characteristics of the location of the schools.

Conclusion

The available evidence from the literature suggests that a lack of basic infrastructure amenities in schools may affect student learning negatively. Given that this study explores questions related to basic school infrastructure needs, costs, and investments in Paraguay, it makes sense to start with a basic diagnostic of the state of infrastructure in public primary and secondary schools. This analysis was based on data from a 2008 school census, and it suggests that while some schools have the infrastructure amenities they need, many do not, especially in rural and poorer areas. In addition in the case of toilets and classrooms, a substantial share of facilities appears to be in poor condition. Finally, new construction at the time of the census, while appropriately focused on classrooms and toilets, appears to have been limited.

Overall, Paraguay's school infrastructure appears to be wanting, and it tends to be less well developed than that of other Latin American countries. In general, areas with higher levels of unmet basic needs as well as rural areas have a lower aggregate index of infrastructure quality, and differences are also observed between departments. While none of these findings are surprising, they help set the stage for more detailed analysis in subsequent chapters.

CHAPTER 3

Budget Allocations and Funding Needs for School Infrastructure

Abstract

As suggested in the basic school infrastructure diagnostic provided in chapter 2, basic infrastructure in Paraguay's public schools at the primary and secondary levels is not as good as it should be. In this context, the objective of this chapter is twofold. First, trends in past budget allocations to basic school infrastructure are discussed, showing that there has been a sharp reduction in such allocations in recent years. Second, given that Paraguay has adopted standards for what schools should have as infrastructure amenities, the cost of fulfilling these requirements is estimated. Given that this cost is found to be very high and beyond reach, alternative suggestions are made for prioritizing basic infrastructure investments, and the cost of these alternative rules is also estimated.

Introduction

A key finding from the previous chapter is that in Paraguay (as in many other developing countries), basic infrastructure in public schools at the primary and secondary levels is not as good as it should be. The share of gross domestic product (GDP) allocated to public spending for education in Paraguay has declined substantially over time. Today, public spending for education appears to be insufficient and is also well below what some other Latin American countries are investing, especially in terms of spending levels per student. At the same time, financial resources are lacking in the public budget in order to be able to rapidly and significantly upgrade this infrastructure. Capital investments appear to be especially constrained in Paraguay, and this makes it necessary to arbitrate between various types of valid basic infrastructure funding needs and various types of schools. The objective of this chapter is to provide broad background information on budget trends and funding needs for basic school infrastructure in order to inform the more detailed work in subsequent chapters on which types of infrastructure investments should be given priority and which schools should benefit from such investments in priority.

Resources available for capital investments in basic school infrastructure in Paraguay have been limited for several reasons, as documented by Rivarola and Elías (2013). First, as already mentioned, overall public spending for education tends to be low in Paraguay in comparison to countries such as Argentina, Brazil, and Chile. Second, the share of public education funding allocated to capital investments is low. Third, only part of what is allocated to capital investments is earmarked for construction and equipment. And finally, only part of the funds allocated to construction and equipment are allocated to basic education (from age 6 to age 14) and upper secondary schools (*educacion media*, for children aged 15 to 17). The first contribution of this chapter is to provide a discussion of the various factors that lead to low levels of investments in basic school infrastructure on the basis of data on trends in such investment for the last dozen years.

The second contribution of this chapter is to provide estimates of funding needs for basic public school infrastructure. It was mentioned in chapter 2 that by law, schools are supposed to be equipped with a wide range of amenities. These standards apply to all public primary and secondary schools. Yet, it is unrealistic to expect that Paraguay will be able to equip all its schools with the amenities identified by Ministry of Education and Culture (MEC) in Decree 6589 and Resolution 3985. Using data from the 2008 Paraguay school infrastructure census, Rivarola and Elías (2013) estimated that the cost of providing the necessary infrastructure would be at least US$ 1.2 billion, which is almost 50 times the total 2012 funding in the education budget for capital investments and almost 500 times the 2012 budget allocated to construction and equipment for schools. This estimate covers the cost of number of amenities, but in fact not all costs for all of the amenities required under the decree were included, so that the estimate is a lower bound. Of course, it does not make sense to equip a small rural primary public school with features such as a direction room or a full laboratory, and this would never be attempted by the MEC. But if the letter of the law were to be followed, the order of magnitude of the costs would simply be staggering.

Given this reality, the second objective of this chapter is to first provide slightly revised estimates of the cost of following the letter of the law (including classroom costs, which was not done by Rivarola and Elías (2013), but is important, given that as shown in chapter 4, classrooms are likely to be the most important investments to make). Next, alternative estimates of the potential cost of basic infrastructure investments under different rules are provided, so as to generate alternatives to the "all or nothing" scenario presented by Rivarola and Elías (2013).

The structure of the chapter is as follows. The next section discusses trends in budget allocations for basic school infrastructure in Paraguay. Next various estimates of funding requirements to improve this infrastructure are provided. Next various estimates provides various estimates of funding requirements to improve this infrastructure. A brief conclusion follows.

Budget Allocations for School Infrastructure

As mentioned in the previous chapter, the share of public education spending for education in GDP decreased from 5.2 percent in 1999 to 4.1 percent in 2010, while other countries have ramped up their own investments in education. As reported by Rivarola and Elías (2013), in the area of investments for basic school infrastructure (construction and equipment), the situation is worse, but this is actually not because of a lack of overall investments or capital expenditures. As shown in figure 3.1, which provides trends in public capital investments in education in Paraguay in real terms (in 2012 Guaranies values), capital investments as allocated in the budget have been decreasing, but not by a large amount. If one abstracts from the peaks in 2000 and 2006, the trend is relatively flat. Furthermore, investments in construction and equipment, which constitutes a subset of capital investments, have increased in recent years.

The issue, as shown in figure 3.2, is that within the broad category of investments in construction and equipment, investments allocated specifically to construction and equipment for basic education schools and upper secondary schools (*educación media*) have been declining over time, especially in recent years. Most of the funding for construction and equipment in recent years has been allocated to tertiary education, improvements in the offices of the Ministry of Education and Culture, and repairs for the *Instituto Superior de Bellas Artes*, among others. Thus, while overall investments in construction and equipment have increased in real terms, the extent to which basic education schools and upper secondary schools have benefitted from those investments has been decreased quite substantially, leading to important needs not being met.

Figure 3.1 Budget for Investment and Construction and Equipment, 2012 PYG

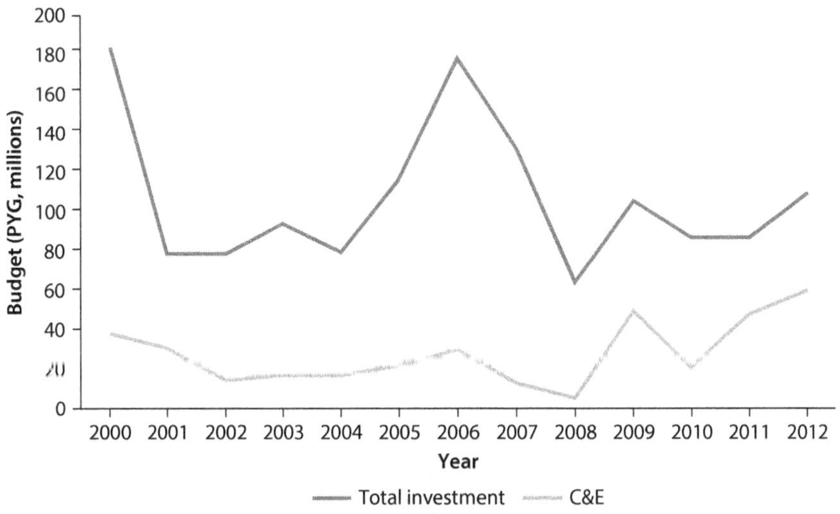

Source: Administrative data from Education Ministry available in Rivarola and Elías (2013).
Note: Estimates are provided in real terms (in 2012 PYG values). C&E = construction and equipment; PYG = Paraguay guaraní.

As a result, as shown in figure 3.3, the Ministry of Education and Culture budget shares allocated to construction and equipment for basic education schools and upper secondary schools have been steadily decreasing over time. Between 1999 and 2010, the share of the total education budget allocated to

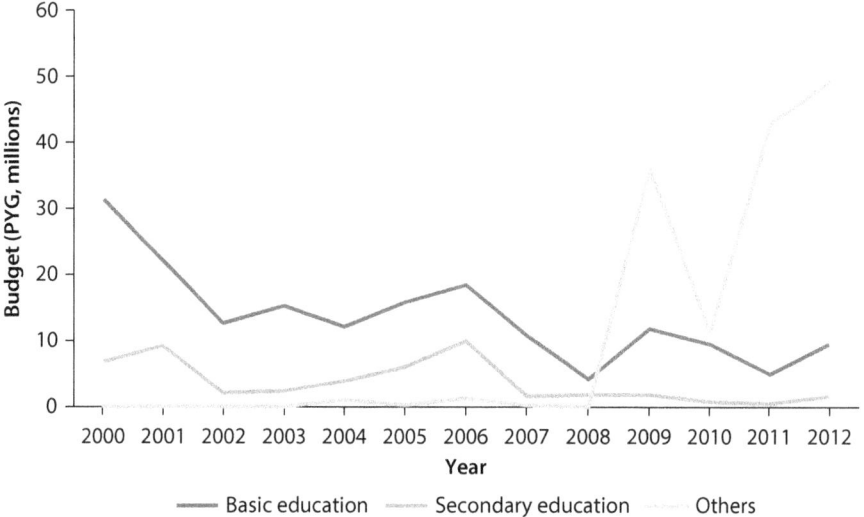

Figure 3.2 Budget for Construction and Equipment in Basic and Upper Secondary Education, 2012 PYG

Source: Administrative data from Education Ministry available in Rivarola and Elías (2013).
Note: Estimates are provided in real terms (in 2012 PYG values). PYG = Paraguay guaraní.

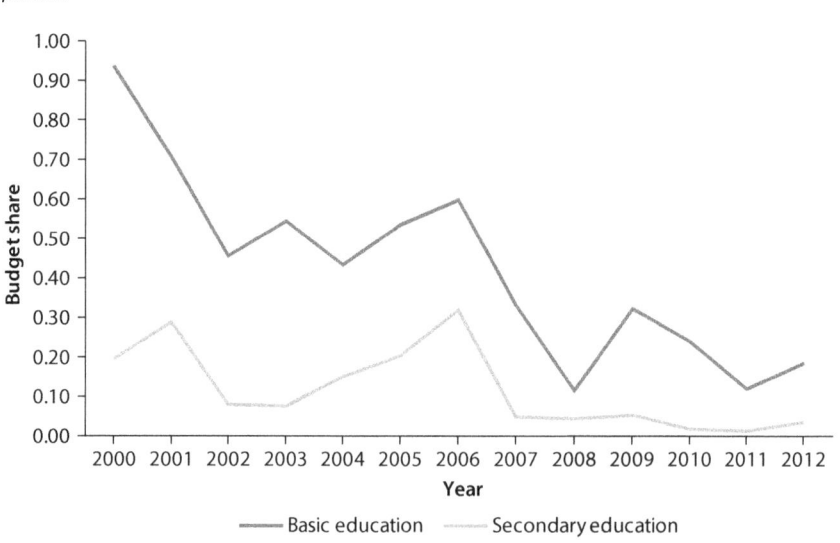

Figure 3.3 Budget Shares for Construction and Equipment
percent

Source: Based on data from Education Ministry in Rivarola and Elías (2013).

construction and equipment in basic education decreased from about 1 percent to one fifth of a percent. The corresponding budget share for construction and equipment for upper secondary school decreased from one fifth of a percent to one twenty fifth of a percent.

Decomposition of Budget Shares for Basic School Infrastructure

In order to analyse in more details the trend in budgetary allocations for basic school infrastructure investments, a simple multiplicative decomposition can be used to identify the sources of the decline over time in the share of the education budget allocated to investments in construction and equipment for basic and lower secondary education. Another measure that is also informative is the share of national GDP that is allocated to such investments.

Define the budget allocated to investments in construction and equipment for basic education as B_{CBE}. As a share of GDP, the budget share is $S_{CBE}=B_{CBE}/GDP$. On the basis of data on (i) public education spending as a share of GDP, denoted by S_E; (ii) The share of public spending on education allocated to investment spending $S_{I|E}$; (iii) the share of investment spending allocated to construction and equipment $S_{CE|I}$; and finally (iv) the share of the budget for construction and equipment allocated to basic education $S_{BE|CE}$, we have the identity:

$$S_{CBE} = S_E \times S_{I|E} \times S_{CE|I} \times S_{BE|CE} \qquad (3.1)$$

The same identity holds for upper secondary schools, with the subscript B for basic can be replaced by the subscript S for upper secondary education in the notation (this is done in table 3.1). If one is interested in measuring the share of the education budget allocated to construction and equipment for basic education, to be denoted by $S_{CBE|E}$ (these are the shares displayed in figure 3.3 for basic education and upper secondary schools), as opposed to the share of GDP allocated for this purpose, the same decomposition applies simply without the first term:

$$S_{CBE|E} = S_{I|E} \times S_{CE|I} \times S_{BE|CE} \qquad (3.2)$$

In equations (3.1) and (3.2), the use of the conditional symbol "|" indicates that each additional share is computed within the funding envelope generated by the previous share(s). For upper secondary school, the same applies and the share of GDP allocated to construction and equipment will be denoted by S_{CSE}, with the same notation applying for the other shares. The potential usefulness of decomposition (3.1) is that it highlights four different ways through which funding for school infrastructure investments in basic education may increase or decrease, namely through changes in the share of GDP allocated to public education spending, the share of public education spending to capital investments, the share of capital investments allocated to construction and equipment, and the share of the construction and equipment budget allocated to basic and secondary education. The same logic applies to decomposition (3.2).

Table 3.1 Budgets and Budget Shares Allocated to Basic School Infrastructure Investments

	2000	2001	2002	2003	2004	2005	2006	2007	2008	2009	2010	2011	2012
Budget in nominal terms													
Investment budget	63.3	30.4	33.8	46.4	43.9	69.6	117.5	92.5	49.6	89.2	74.8	79.5	109.6
Construction and equipment	13.1	12	6.3	8.5	9.3	13.1	19.6	8.8	4.4	41.7	18.2	43.8	60.3
C&E for basic education	10.8	8.5	5.4	7.5	6.6	9.4	12.2	7.6	3.1	9.9	8.0	4.4	9.4
C&E for secondary education	2.3	3.5	0.9	1.1	2.2	3.6	6.6	1.1	1.3	1.5	0.6	0.3	1.6
GDP deflator													
Change in GDP deflator	11.7	11.0	14.9	12.2	9.0	10.1	6.1	9.8	9.3	2.0	6.1	9.8	4.6
GDP deflator index, 2012 base	290.2	259.8	234.1	203.7	181.6	166.6	151.3	142.6	129.9	118.8	116.5	109.8	100.0
Budget in real terms, 2012 value													
Investment budget	183.7	79.0	79.1	94.5	79.7	115.9	177.8	131.9	64.4	106.0	87.1	87.3	109.6
Construction and equipment	38.0	31.2	14.7	17.3	16.9	21.8	29.7	12.5	5.7	49.6	21.2	48.1	60.3
C&E for basic education	31.3	22.1	12.6	15.3	12.0	15.7	18.5	10.8	4.0	11.8	9.3	4.8	9.4
C&E for secondary education	6.7	9.1	2.1	2.2	4.0	6.0	10.0	1.6	1.7	1.8	0.7	0.3	1.6
Shares vs. Education budget													
S_{IJE}	5.5	2.5	2.9	3.4	2.9	4.0	5.8	4.0	1.8	2.9	2.2	2.2	2.1
$S_{CB|J}$	20.7	39.5	18.6	18.3	21.2	18.8	16.7	9.5	8.9	46.7	24.3	55.1	55.0
$S_{BE|CB}$	82	71	85	88	70	71	62	87	71	24	44	10	16
$S_{SE|CB}$	17	29	15	12	24	27	33	13	28	4	3	1	3
$S_{CBE|E}$	0.94	0.71	0.45	0.55	0.43	0.54	0.60	0.33	0.11	0.32	0.24	0.12	0.19
$S_{CSE|E}$	0.19	0.29	0.08	0.07	0.15	0.20	0.32	0.05	0.04	0.05	0.02	0.01	0.04
Shares vs. national GDP													
S_E	5.3	5.1	4.9	4.7	4	—	—	4	—	—	4.1	—	4.1[a]
S_{CBE}	0.050	0.036	0.022	0.026	0.017	—	—	0.013	—	—	0.010	—	0.008[a]
S_{CSE}	0.010	0.015	0.004	0.004	0.006	—	—	0.002	—	—	0.001	—	0.001[a]

Source: Author's estimations from administrative data available in Rivarola and Elias (2013), except for the share of public education spending in GDP (SE), which is obtained from the UNESCO database and the GDP deflator obtained from the World Bank's World Development Indicators database.

Note: C&E = construction and equipment; GDP = gross domestic product; — = not available.

a. The decomposition of construction and equipment spending as a share of GDP is provided in the table for 2012 under the assumption that the share of the public education budget in GDP in 2012 is similar to that observed in 2010.

The various shares are provided in table 3.1, together with the data in both nominal and real terms on budget allocations for investments, for construction and equipment within investments, and for construction and equipment for basic education and upper secondary schools separately. Note that presenting the data in real terms using Paraguay's GDP deflator makes a substantial difference versus data in nominal terms since inflation has been very substantial over time.

As mentioned in the previous section, the shares of the public spending for education allocated to construction and equipment in basic and upper secondary education were both reduced fivefold between 2000 and 2012, from about 1 percent to one fifth of a percent in the case of basic education and from one fifth of a percent to one twenty fifth of a percent for upper secondary schools. The reductions are even sharper when considering the shares of GDP allocated to construction and equipment for basic and upper secondary schools. The reductions in shares take place for the most part after 2006, with different dates from the various reductions, although the reduction in the share of GDP allocated to public spending in education is observed earlier.

Importantly, not all of the changes in parameters in equation (3.1) go in the same direction. There was a reduction after 2004 in S_E, the share of public education spending in GDP, and there was also a reduction in $S_{I|E}$, the share of public spending on education allocated to investment spending, especially as of 2008. On the other hand, the share of investment spending allocated to construction and equipment $S_{CE|I}$, increased as of 2009. But as already mentioned, the share of the budget for construction and equipment allocated to basic education, $S_{BE|CE}$, decreased sharply as of 2009, and the same was observed for and upper secondary education, $S_{SE|CE}$.

Since the decompositions (3.1) and (3.2) are multiplicative, for small enough changes in shares, the proportional change over time in budget shares can be approximated in additive terms, as follows for decomposition (3.1) and without the first term for decomposition (3.2):

$$\Delta S_{CBE} / S_{CBE} = (S_{CBE}^{t+1} - S_{CBE}^{t}) / S_{CBE}^{t} \approx (\ln S_E^{t+1} - \ln S_E^{t}) \\ + (\ln S_{I|E}^{t+1} - \ln S_{I|E}^{t}) + (\ln S_{CE|I}^{t+1} - \ln S_{CE|I}^{t}) + (\ln S_{BE|CE}^{t+1} - \ln S_{BE|CE}^{t}) \quad (3.3)$$

This approximation is valid only for small enough changes in shares. In table 3.1, changes in shares tend to be large, so the approximation is not always precise when looking at changes from year to year. But an alternative is to look at changes over time on the basis of annual rates of changes for the various shares. This is done in table 3.2 for the period 2000–12 under the assumption that the share of the public education budget in GDP was similar in 2012 to the value for 2010, the latest year of data on that share (see the note in table 3.1). Under that assumption, the annual rate of change in the construction and equipment budget for basic education as a share of GDP between 2000 and 2012 was –14.4 percent, implying that every year, the allocated budget decreased on average by

Table 3.2 Decomposition of Average Rates of Year-on-year Changes in Budget Shares

	Basic education (%)	Upper secondary (%)
(1) Annual rate of change in C&E budget for schools as a share of GDP	−14.4	−15.1
(2) Annual rate of change in education spending as a share of GDP	−2.1	−2.1
(3) Annual rate of change in investment share in public education spending	−7.6	−7.6
(4) Annual rate of change in C&E budget share in education investments	8.5	8.5
(5) Annual rate of change in C&E budget share for schools in total C&E budget	−12.7	−13.5
Memo: Sum of the contributions (2) through (5), noting that (1) ≈ (2)+(3)+(4)+(5)	−14.0	−14.7

Source: Author's estimations.
Note: the annual rate of change is the compounded year-on-year change estimated through a power function; it is not the cumulative change between the initial and final years divided by the number of years between the two dates.

that proportion versus the previous year. For upper education, the annual rate of decrease in the construction and equipment budget as a share of GDP was slightly larger, at 15.1 percent. In turn, these rates of decline can be decomposed in various contributions.

The reduction in public education spending as a share of GDP contributed for 2.1 percentage points to the overall average annual decline over the period of 14.4 percentage points. The reduction in investments as a share of education spending contributed another 7.6 percentage points decline. Because construction and equipment spending as a whole increased as a share of investment spending, this contributed to an average increase in the budget share of 8.5 percent. But the decrease in spending for construction and equipment specifically for basic education within the overall construction and equipment envelope yielded another 12.7 percentage point decline on average over the period. The findings are broadly similar for upper secondary schools. If one is interested in trends in budget allocations for school construction and equipment as a share of public education spending, the same decomposition applies, but without the first term, which relates to the change in the education budget as a share of GDP.

While this decomposition is nothing but another way to present the basic data already available in table 3.1, it may help in assessing over time the magnitude of the various effects at play in the overall decline of construction and equipment allocations for basic education and for upper secondary schools. Overall, the largest effect was that of the allocations within the budget for construction and equipment to the detriment of basic and upper secondary education.

Before concluding this section, as noted by Rivarola and Elías (2013), one should point out that other sources of funding for investments in basic school infrastructure not included in the budget may have been available from donors. Taking into account these data could change the overall assessment of the trend in allocations for school construction and equipment for the better, but the data available to the author are not detailed enough to conduct this assessment.

Funding Needs for School Infrastructure

School Amenities

The analysis now turns to assessing funding needs for basic infrastructure investments. As noted in the introduction to this chapter, the Ministry of Education and Culture's Decree 6589 and Resolution 3985 stipulate that all schools should have a number of basic amenities. On the basis of data from the 2008 Paraguay school infrastructure census, Rivarola and Elías (2013) computed the cost of fulfilling this mandate. The cost calculations are straightforward—one simply needs to multiply unit costs for basic amenities (as provided in table 3.2 on the basis of estimates obtained for Paraguay) by the number of schools that need each type of amenity.

Under the baseline scenario in table 3.3, which corresponds to the estimates by Rivarola and Elías (2013), all schools that require an amenity are provided with that amenity regardless of their size and whether they are primary or secondary schools. The total baseline cost in table 3.2 is ₲5,134 billion (this differs very slightly from the cost computed by Rivarola and Elías in part because we did not include toilets, as it is assumed here that this would be included in sanitation facilities, but the order of magnitude is similar). This corresponds to US$ 1.2 billion at current exchange rates (in August 2013, 1 PYG = 0.00023 US$) and is equivalent to 47 times the 2012 funding in the education budget for capital investments as a whole, 85 times the 2012 budget for construction and equipment, and 468 times the combined construction and equipment budget allocated in 2012 to basic education and upper secondary schools. This estimate covers the cost of providing toilets/bathrooms, a direction room, a secretarial room, a library, a laboratory, a multiuse room, a room for teachers, and a sports and recreation room in all public primary and secondary public schools identified in the 2008 census that do not have these amenities. With a total of 6,608 public schools, this represents an average investment of US$ 182,000 per school.

As noted in the introduction, this estimate is actually a lower bound of the full cost of implementing the decree without distinctions between schools, as a number of amenities were not included in the estimation due to lack of unit cost estimates. For example, the cost of providing electricity and water to the schools that do not have these amenities was not included. In addition, the cost of providing the number of classrooms in principle required for each school and the cost of decongesting schools that have the minimum number of classrooms required but are now crowded (thereby requiring additional classrooms) were not included.

Table 3.3 Estimation of the Potential Budgetary Cost of Selected Basic Amenities for Paraguay's Schools

Amenities	Baseline share of schools served (%)	Baseline share of students served (%)	Unit cost per school (PYG millions)	All schools (no conditions on size or secondary school)				Median threshold and secondary school conditions for laboratories and multiuse rooms						Unit cost ratio for median vs. all
				Number needed	Cost (PYG billions)	Students served (%)	Cost per additional student served (₲1,000)	Median size threshold	Number needed	Cost (PYG billions)	Students served (%)	Cost per additional student served (₲1,000)	Share of gap filled (%)	
Costs														
Direction room	43.5	68.0	42.5	3,732	158.6	100.0	447.8	161	556	23.6	82.2	150.4	44.4	0.336
Secretarial room	12.1	33.7	42.5	5,809	246.9	100.0	336.5	317	425	18.1	53.5	82.4	29.9	0.245
Library	13.8	36.1	75.1	5,694	427.6	100.0	604.7	299.5	436	32.7	56.1	147.9	31.3	0.245
Laboratory	3.2	12.6	145.6	6,396	931.3	100.0	962.7	457	382	55.6	38.4	194.8	29.5	0.202
Multiuse room	3.8	10.4	145.6	6,355	925.3	100.0	933.1	246	1,051	153.0	57.6	292.9	52.7	0.314
Teachers' room	5.7	18.2	84.9	6,229	528.8	100.0	584.1	368	806	68.4	55.3	166.7	45.4	0.285
Recreation area	3.6	12.9	287.0	6,372	1,828.8	100.0	1,897.1	426	428	122.8	40.4	403.6	31.6	0.213
Sanitation	56.4	74.2	30.1	2,880	86.7	100.0	303.6	129	661	19.9	88.8	123.1	56.6	0.406
Total cost														
Billions PYG					5,134.0					494.2				
Million US$					1,180.8					113.7				

Source: Author's estimations.
Note: PYG = Paraguay guaraní.

In this section, alternative estimates of the potential cost of school infrastructure investments are provided through restrictions on the number of schools that can benefit from amenities. That is, instead of providing all amenities to all school, rules are used to target some of the larger schools for the amenities, and the cost of providing the amenities is then computed under those rules. Many different rules or formulas could be used for targeting larger school. Just as an example of a potential approach, the following rule is used: each amenity is provided only to schools that lack the amenity and have a number of students higher than the median number of students among the schools that have the amenity. Presumably, previous allocations were made under some guidelines as to which schools should benefit from various amenities, with larger schools provided with more amenities. Using the median size of the schools that have an amenity is one way to suggest which schools should benefit from an amenity in priority.

A more requiring threshold would be to provide improvements, say, only to schools that have a student population higher than the 75th percentile of the schools with a given amenity. All such thresholds are clearly arbitrary, but the interesting question is whether a substantial reduction in the number of schools to be served under such rules is achieved and whether this has a large negative effect on the number of students served or not. Also of interest is the cost per additional student served under various rules. By targeting in priority larger schools, the cost of infrastructure improvements per student served will be lower in those schools. This also means that within a necessarily limited budget envelope, targeting larger schools means that the number of students who will benefit from improvements will be larger. The question is whether the magnitude of these various effects tends to be small, or large. For example, under the median rule just described, does the cost per student of providing amenities decrease by 20 percent, or is it cut in half? And what is the loss in terms of the coverage of the student population?

In addition to the median rule used to target larger schools for each type of amenity, it is likely that some amenities will matter more in secondary than in primary schools. Laboratories and multiuse rooms come to mind, given that their use in primary schools is likely to be limited. For those two amenities, only secondary schools are considered as potential beneficiaries.

The results of the alternative simulation are provided in table 3.3. The first two columns provide information on the share of schools that have an amenity, and the share of students in schools with the amenity (if an amenity is rated by the school's administrator as in poor condition, the school is considered as not having that amenity, given that repairs, or a new amenity, are likely to be required—this affects only a minority of school in most cases). Because larger schools have more amenities, the share of students benefitting from each amenity is larger than the corresponding share of schools with the amenity. The third column provides the unit investment costs for the various amenities. The next set of columns provides estimates of the investment needed to provide all the amenities to all schools.

The results from the application of the median and secondary school rules for some amenities are provided next. Under the median rule and the additional requirement to provide laboratories and multiuse rooms only to secondary schools, the estimated cost of provision is reduced more than tenfold, from ₲5,134.0 billions under the baseline to ₲494.2 billions. The loss in coverage, while important, is less severe. The share of the gap-filled column indicates the share of the students who previously did not study in a school with an amenity, but now do, benefit from the amenity. This share varies by amenity from 29.5 percent for laboratories (note that this includes many primary school students) to 56.6 percent for sanitation. Thus, between one third and half of the students remain served at less than one tenth of the cost. As expected, the unit cost per student of providing amenities is also much lower under the alternative scenario than under the baseline. The ratios of average unit costs per additional student served vary from 0.202 for laboratories to 0.406 for sanitation, suggesting that on average, unit costs per additional student served are reduced by a factor of about three when using the median rule together with the restriction for some amenities to be provided only to secondary schools.

Classrooms

It was mentioned earlier that the cost of providing additional classrooms to schools that need them was not included in the cost simulation carried by Rivarola and Elías (2013). Because classrooms do matter (as discussed in more details in chapter 4), and more so than most other amenities, it is useful to also provide estimates of the potential cost of providing classrooms to the schools that need them. The approach to do so is however slightly different, given that for classrooms it is not a matter of providing one or no classroom as is the case for the other amenities, but rather a matter of how many classrooms should be provided, which depends on a school's number of students and number of available classrooms (as for other amenities, we consider as available only classrooms that are not in poor condition).

As was done in chapter 2, denote by y_i the number of classrooms available in a school normalized by the number of classrooms that should be available so that a value of 100 means that the school has exactly the number of classrooms it needs, given its student population (all schools with an index value at or above 100 are not infrastructure poor). If one considers a benchmark baseline case in which one classroom should be available per set of $n = 30$ students in a school (additional benchmarks of $n = 25$ and $n = 20$ will be considered), and if one denotes by CU_i the number of classrooms in use in a school (this information is available in the census) and by P_i and S_i the number of primary and secondary students, then the index CAI_i is defined as follows:

$$CAI_i = \frac{CU_i \times n \times 100}{P_i + S_i} \quad \text{with} \quad n = 20, 25, 30 \tag{3.4}$$

The value of n can be changed to assess the cost implications of different classroom norms, and for any given value for n, one can compute from the 2008 school census database the number of additional classrooms that would be needed in order to ensure that the value of y_i is above 100 for all schools (if $n = 30$, if a school has 31 students and one classroom, it will require a second classroom in the way in which the estimates provided below are computed; relaxing this assumption would require fewer classrooms to be built, so that the cost estimates provided are indicative only). Apart from this norm, a second norm in Paraguay is that in principle all schools should have at least one classroom per grade taught. This would mean that all primary schools would need at least six classrooms, and the same would hold for secondary schools. One could challenge this rule, since at least in small rural primary schools the cost of implementing the rule is likely to be much higher than relying on multigrade teaching, and the rule does not seem to be applied in practice. But as was the case for amenities, assessing the cost and funding needs simulations provided in this chapter under that theoretical rule is useful to compare this cost with more practical rules based on a comparison of available classrooms per students.

Table 3.4 provides the results of the various computations. When the requirement of having at least six classrooms per school is imposed (it is assumed here that all schools teach to at least six grades), the number of new classrooms to be built is very high, and so are the budgetary costs (the cost of a classroom with all required equipment is estimated at ₲62,926,731 or US$ 14,473). Without the requirement of at least six classrooms per school, the number of classrooms required is lower but still significant. In the baseline

Table 3.4 Potential Budgetary Cost of New Classrooms for Paraguay's Schools

Scenario	Average number of classrooms needed per school	Total number of classrooms needed	Budgetary cost (PYG billions)	Budgetary cost (US$ millions)
With requirement to have one classroom per grade				
$n = 20$	4.6	30,177	1,899.4	436.9
$n = 25$	3.4	22,161	1,394.5	320.7
$n = 30$ (baseline)	2.7	17,526	1,102.9	253.7
Without requirement to have one classroom per grade				
$n = 20$	3.3	22,097	1,390.5	319.8
$n = 25$	2.0	13.245	833.5	191.7
$n = 30$ (baseline)	1.2	8,134	511.8	117.7

Source: Author's estimations.
Note: The unit cost per classroom with all required equipment is assumed to be ₲ 62,926,731 or US$ 14,473.
PYG = Paraguay guaraní.

scenario with $n = 30$ and no minimum number of classrooms per school, 8,134 new classrooms would be required at a cost of ₲511.8 billion or US$ 117.7 million. This cost would be of the same order of magnitude as the cost for the other school amenities discussed in the previous section under the median rule and the limitations of laboratories and multiuse classrooms to secondary schools. It is also worth noting that in its micro-planning exercise for 2013, the Ministry of Education and Culture estimated that a total of 7,076 classrooms would have to be built, and another 6,220 repaired.

Conclusion

The first objective of this chapter was to review recent trends in budget allocations to basic school infrastructure in Paraguay. The analysis suggests that due to various factors, there has been a sharp reduction in these allocations in recent years. This reduction is likely to have contributed at least in part to the poor state of basic infrastructure in schools documented in chapter 2. The second objective of the chapter was to give an indication of potential funding needs for school infrastructure. While standards have been adopted in many countries as to what each and every school should have as a minimum, such standards will be useful only to the extent that they are realistic. In Paraguay, the requirement that all primary and secondary schools be equipped with (among others) direction and secretarial rooms, as well as one classroom per grade, a room for recreation and physical education, a library, and a laboratory, is simply overly ambitious. The cost of providing these amenities would be much too high, especially in a context where budget allocations for school construction and equipment have been substantially reduced.

Rather than aiming to equip all schools with as many amenities as possible, a better approach is to try to allocate amenities and classrooms where they appear to most needed. Illustrations of how this could be done have been provided in this chapter. Again, this analysis and these estimates are ad hoc, and different assumptions could be used in terms of the targets to be reached as well as the unit costs to be considered. Different budget estimates will then be associated with different rules for types of amenities whereby only larger schools and/or secondary school would be considered in need of specific amenities. Similarly, different assumptions about classroom needs could be used, leading to different cost estimates. Even the more restrictive scenarios presented in the chapter result in very high cost estimates in comparison to what is currently allocated for school construction and equipment. It is nevertheless hoped that this type of basic analysis helps in getting at least an order of magnitude of what investment costs might have to be contemplated under various allocation rules, given that providing all amenities and many classrooms to all schools is neither feasible nor cost efficient.

CHAPTER 4

Primary School Infrastructure and Student Performance

Abstract

The education literature suggests that better basic infrastructure in schools is likely to contribute to improvements in student learning. However, which investments are the most likely to improve student performance in any specific country is often less clear. Paraguay has adopted standards that recommend that all schools benefit from a wide range of infrastructure investments. As discussed in chapter 3, this approach unfortunately is not very helpful, because the cost of such upgrades may rapidly become prohibitive. Finding ways to prioritize investments seems more promising. On the basis of the estimation of an education production function, this chapter suggests that in Paraguay, investments in classrooms and access to electricity are likely to bring larger gains than other investments. Furthermore, in the case of classrooms, the largest gains are observed when investing in the schools that are the most crowded in terms of lack of classrooms.

Introduction

The literature on education production functions suggests that a lack of basic amenities and other school inputs affects student learning negatively. There has been a debate about the magnitude of those effects. One of the first studies in the field (Coleman et al. 1966) suggested that family background and peers had a much larger impact on achievement than school inputs. Over the last three decades, Hanushek (for example, 1986, 2010; see Hanushek and Woessmann 2011) has argued that education provision is inefficient and that most school inputs make only at best a small difference in achievement. For example, Hanushek recognizes that teacher quality matters, but he suggests that teacher quality is often not related to pay or formal qualifications. But the view that somehow inputs do not matter much has been challenged. For example, in their meta-analyses of education studies, Card and Krueger (1992) as well as Greenwald, Hedges, and Laine (1996) do find that school resources tend to be positively associated with earnings and educational attainment, a conclusion also reached in a recent review by Baker (2012). The in-depth review of education production functions completed by Glewwe et al. (2013) also suggests that the availability of basic furniture (desks, tables, and chairs), electricity, school libraries, and high-quality walls, roofs, and floors all have positive impacts on learning.

While investments in school infrastructure help, identifying exactly which investments are most likely to improve student performance in any specific country is more difficult, since this depends on the country's circumstances and previous investments in school infrastructure. In the absence of detailed analyses of what works best, some countries have adopted standards that recommend that all schools benefit from a wide range of infrastructure investments.

In Paraguay, the right to a free public basic education is enshrined in the National Constitution of 1992. The General Education Law of 1998 further states that the whole population should have equal access to education, and the article 141 of the law states that the Ministry of Education and Culture (MEC) must ensure that all schools meet minimum criteria in terms of infrastructure, pedagogy, administration, and financing. In its 1999 Decree 6589 and through Resolution 3985, MEC established standards for all schools providing basic education. According to those standards, all schools should have (i) a direction room; (ii) a secretarial room; (iii) at least one classroom (7.2 meter × 7.2 meter) per grade with proper ventilation and light; (iv) separate bathrooms for boys and girls; (v) a proper space for recreation and physical education; (vi) drinking water; and (vii) a library. In addition, each school should also have a laboratory for physics, chemistry, and the natural sciences (Rivarola and Elias 2013).

While establishing such standards may reflect aspirations, it may not be that helpful in a country such as Paraguay. Previous studies as well as the estimations in chapter 2 suggest that even the most basic infrastructure is often lacking in Paraguay's schools, and chapter 3 has demonstrated that budgets are insufficient to improve the situation without strict prioritization (Brizuela 2008; Rivarola and Elías 2013). In comparison to other Latin American countries, Paraguay is one of the countries with the largest school infrastructure deficits (Duarte, Gargiulo, and Moreno 2011; Murillo and Román 2011). Because so many schools lack most of the features identified by the MEC standards as required, the cost of providing these features to all the schools would simply be prohibitive. Said differently, those aspirations are not realistic even in the medium term and therefore not really useful for selecting the priority investments that must be made.

In this context, the objective of this chapter is to assess which infrastructure inputs are likely to make the largest difference for success (passing rates) in public primary schools. This is done by estimating an education production function using data from a school census. The results suggest that in the case of Paraguay, investments in classrooms and access to electricity would probably bring larger gains than other investments, including those identified as required for schools in the standards of the MEC. Furthermore, in the case of classrooms, the estimations also suggest that the largest gains in passing rates would likely be observed when investing in the schools that are the most crowded in terms of the lack of classrooms.

In what follows, the next section outlines the methodology and provides summary statistics for the variables of interest. The following section provides the regression analysis. A conclusion follows.

Methodology and Summary Statistics

This section has two objectives. The first is to very briefly show that it is unrealistic to expect that Paraguay will be able to equip all its schools with the amenities identified by MEC in Decree 6589 and Resolution 3985. The second is to present the methodology and data used to identify which infrastructure might lead to the largest gains in passing rates in primary schools.

Consider first the issue of the cost of providing all public schools with the amenities identified by MEC in its standards for public schools. These standards apply to all public primary and secondary schools. Using data from the 2008 Paraguay school infrastructure census on which schools have which amenities, Rivarola and Elías (2013) estimate that the cost of providing the necessary infrastructure would be US$ 1.2 billion, which is equivalent to about 50 times the total available annual funding in the education budget for capital investments. This estimate covers the cost of providing toilets/bathrooms, as well as a direction room, a secretarial room, a library, a laboratory, a multiuse room, a room for teachers, and a sports and recreation room, in all public primary and secondary public schools identified in the 2008 census. With a total of 6,608 public schools, this represents an average investment of US$ 182,000 per school, which is very high. If one were to add the required investments in additional classrooms in order to meet the requirement to have at least one classroom per grade, the cost would be even higher. Of course, it does not make sense to equip a small rural primary public school with all these features, and this would never be actually implemented by the MEC. But if the letter of the law were to be followed, this would be the order of magnitude of the costs.

Clearly, priorities for infrastructure investments in public schools are needed. How can this be done? In the literature, identifying these priorities is typically done through the estimation of education production functions that relate performance measures such as test scores (the dependent variable) or passing rates to various inputs (the independent variables). Inputs directly controlled by policy makers include school and teacher characteristics as well as curricula. Other inputs include the characteristics of the student's households and peers. When student data are available, these education production functions can be estimated at the level of students. But they can also be estimated at the level of schools using average test scores or passing rates.

A recent review by Glewwe et al. (2013) of some of the better estimations of production functions suggests that the availability of basic infrastructure in schools does matter for student learning. The authors review a set of 79 good studies, 43 of which are deemed to be of high quality. Table 4.1 provides the key results from the review as it relates to basic school infrastructure. In the table, the main figures are the number of estimates available in the studies pointing to a particular relationship (positive, neutral, or negative) between inputs and student learning. The figures in parentheses are the number of papers or studies from which the estimates are drawn (some papers may have different sets of estimates from different regressions). The evidence suggests that textbooks and similar materials do increase student learning, albeit to a lesser extent than is often believed in that few impact estimates are both positive and statistically significant. The availability of basic furniture (desks, tables, and chairs) does seem to have a more systematic positive effect, but this is not the case for computers and other electronics. Electricity seems to play a positive role, as do school libraries and high-quality walls, roofs, and floors. Overall, it does appear that basic school infrastructure has a positive impact on learning.

Table 4.1 Impact on Test Scores of School Infrastructure and Pedagogical Supplies

	Negative			Positive		
	Significant	Insignificant	Zero, or insignificant and no sign given	Insignificant	Significant	Total studies
79 good-quality studies						
Textbooks/workbooks	4 (3)	13 (8)	7 (5)	10 (7)	26 (10)	21
Desks/tables/chairs	0 (0)	0 (0)	13 (1)	7 (5)	8 (4)	8
Computers/electronics	1 (1)	9 (5)	1 (1)	8 (3)	7 (4)	8
Electricity	0 (0)	3 (2)	0 (0)	6 (5)	6 (2)	6
School infr. index	0 (0)	1 (1)	7 (1)	1 (1)	13 (4)	6
Blackboard/flip chart	0 (0)	2 (2)	13 (1)	3 (3)	7 (3)	6
Library	1 (1)	3 (2)	7 (1)	1 (1)	10 (5)	6
Roof/wall/floor	0 (0)	1 (1)	0 (0)	3 (2)	2 (1)	4
43 high-quality studies						
Textbooks/workbooks	1 (1)	8 (4)	3 (1)	6 (4)	3 (2)	8
Desks/tables/chairs	0 (0)	0 (0)	0 (0)	4 (3)	3 (2)	4
Computers/electronics	1 (1)	9 (5)	0 (0)	8 (3)	4 (3)	6
Electricity	0 (0)	3 (2)	0 (0)	3 (2)	0 (0)	3
Blackboard/flip chart	0 (0)	2 (2)	0 (0)	2 (2)	2 (1)	3
Library	0 (0)	1 (1)	0 (0)	1 (1)	4 (2)	3
Roof/wall/floor	0 (0)	1 (1)	0 (0)	3 (2)	2 (1)	4

Source: Glewwe et al. 2013.
Note: Figures are number of estimates; figures in parentheses are number of papers/studies. Table includes all school infrastructure characteristics with at least two separate papers/studies.

As noted by Glewwe et al. (2013), estimating education production functions is not easy because of the risks of omitted variable bias, sample selection, endogenous program placement, and measurement errors. When key variables are omitted from the regressors, the potential correlation between the omitted variables and other regressors will lead to bias in the coefficient estimates. The issue of sample selection relates to the fact that who goes to specific schools is no random, but the results of choices made by parents, and this is often not observed well. Endogenous program placement relates to the fact that some school characteristics may themselves be the result of school performance—one possibility would be that better performing schools are allocated more resources by Ministries of Education, or inversely it could be that less well-performing schools receive more resources to facilitate catch up. Finally, measurement errors may affect both the independent and dependent variables, and they will bias coefficient estimates toward zero due to noise. The fact that when assessing the quality of the estimation of education production functions in the literature, Glewwe et al. (2013) reduced their sample of eligible papers from 307 to only 79 good-quality studies and an even lower 43 high-quality studies shows how difficult it is to correct for these various potential sources of bias.

In this chapter, a school-level education production function is estimated for primary public schools. The outcome variable is the passing rate of the school. The independent variables are a series of infrastructure indicators, as well as other controls including indicators of unmet basic needs in the areas and geographic departmental variables. It should be emphasized that the regressions are likely to suffer from some of the sources of bias just discussed. Omitted variable bias is likely to be present, simply because some of the key inputs such as the pupil–teacher ratio are not observed. Sample selection bias may be observed as well because students self-select in specific schools when they have a choice of school. Endogenous program placement bias is perhaps less likely to be observed, simply because previous research suggests that the allocation of infrastructure investments between schools seems to be ad hoc and based on requests from school principals without any systematic allocation mechanisms (Brizuela 2008). Measurement errors may be present, but probably not more so than is usual with the type of data used. Given the possibility of bias, results should be interpreted with caution, but to the extent that they are robust and reasonable, they provide more information than not relying on any estimation at all.

Table 4.2 provides summary statistics for the variables used in the estimation. Statistics are provided both for all primary schools and for the primary schools that do not also have a secondary school. Because the independent variables are measured at the level of schools, the estimations for the subsample of primary schools that do not also have an associated secondary school are probably more reliable. This is because when a primary school has an associated secondary school, it is not clear whether infrastructure inputs are used more at the primary or secondary level. This problem is not present for schools with primary grades only.

Table 4.2 Summary Statistics for the Variables of Interest, Paraguay 2008 (Not Weighted)

	All primary schools	Primary schools without a secondary school
Passing rate	0.861	0.869
Urban area	0.195	0.087
Combined with secondary school	0.478	n.a.
Classroom availability index		
CAI < 75	0.112	0.038
75 ≤ CAI < 100	0.118	0.055
100 ≤ CAI < 125	0.131	0.090
125 ≤ CAI < 150	0.127	0.114
150 ≤ CAI < 175	0.112	0.125
175 ≤ CAI < 200	0.086	0.094
Other school investments		
Direction room	0.405	0.256
Secretarial room	0.089	0.023
Library	0.116	0.047
Laboratory	0.016	0.001
Workshop room	0.014	0.004
Multiuse room	0.028	0.017
Teachers' room	0.037	0.009
Sanitation index	0.053	0.068
Electricity	0.920	0.862
Piped water	0.413	0.328
Computers	0.208	0.105
Internet access	0.030	0.006
Unmet basic needs		
Unmet basic needs—housing quality	38.930	40.056
Unmet basic needs—access to education	29.918	31.889
Unmet basic needs—livelihoods	16.409	17.325
Department		
Alto Parana	0.097	0.097
Amambay	0.025	0.037
Boquerón	0.006	0.007
Caaguazu	0.118	0.116
Caazapa	0.060	0.064
Canindeyu	0.058	0.056
Capital	0.013	0.003
Central	0.089	0.027
Concepcion	0.056	0.059

table continues next page

Table 4.2 Summary Statistics for the Variables of Interest, Paraguay 2008 (Not Weighted)
(continued)

	All primary schools	Primary schools without a secondary school
Cordillera	0.048	0.051
Guaira	0.049	0.058
Itapua	0.112	0.142
Misiones	0.026	0.028
Paraguari	0.063	0.063
Presidente Hayes	0.025	0.027
Sanpedro	0.127	0.121
Neembucu	0.024	0.040

Source: Estimation using Paraguay 2008 school census.
Note: n.a. = not applicable.

Table 4.2 shows that the average passing grade in the school is at 86.1 percent for all primary schools and 86.9 percent for the primary schools without a secondary school (the statistics in table 4.2 are not weighted by the number of students in each school because the regressions are not weighted either). Close to one fifth of all primary schools are in urban areas, but when considering only primary schools without a secondary school, this drops to less than 10 percent. Close to half of the primary schools have an associated secondary school.

The next variable in table 4.2 is a classroom availability index in the school. Denote as was already done in chapter 2 the index by CAI_i in school i. It is defined as the number of classrooms available in a school normalized by the number of classrooms that should be available so that a value of 100 means that the school has exactly the number of classrooms it needs, given its student population (for this chapter, we consider only primary schools):

$$CAI_i = \frac{CU_i \times n \times 100}{P_i} \quad \text{with} \quad n = 30 \quad (4.1)$$

In equation (4.1), CU_i is the number of classrooms in use in a school and P_i is the number of students in the primary school. The variable n is a normative threshold that represents the number of students that should be associated with each classroom. Given that the standard classroom in Paraguay is supposed to be 7.2 meter by 7.2 meter, only a limited number of students will fit comfortably in any given classroom. The baseline value chosen here is $n = 30$, which means that a school with 150 students should have five classrooms. Using a slightly different normalization (say, $n = 25$) would not affect the regression results significantly.

In table 4.2, schools have been allocated to different interval values for CAI_i, with the first interval set at a value below 75, and then intervals for increases in the index of 25. The reason for using such a specification is that in the regression analysis, it accommodates for potential nonlinearities in the relationship between classroom availability and passing grades in a much better way than a quadratic or other straightjacket functional form would do. For example, this type of specification helps in identifying whether the gains from classroom construction are likely to be higher if classrooms are built in schools that are especially overcrowded. It can be seen that for all primary schools combined, 11.2 percent of the school have a CAI below 75, followed by 11.8 of the schools with a CAI between 75 and 100, and so on. The reference category in the regression is a CAI value above 200, and the proportion of schools that have that value (48.5 percent) can be obtained by subtracting from one all the other values. Note that when considering only primary schools without an associated secondary school, the CAI values tend to be higher, simply because a larger number of those schools are in small rural areas, where there are relatively fewer students per available classroom in many (but not all) cases.

The next set of variables indicate whether schools have a direction room, a secretarial room, a library, a laboratory, a workshop room, a multiuse room, a teachers' room, proper sanitation (the sanitation index is the number of toilets divided by the number of students), electricity, piped water, access to computers, and finally access to the Internet. In the case of the various types of rooms and the toilets, the census data set identifies whether the facilities are in very good, good, or poor condition, and only the facilities in very good or good condition (this is the large majority of the facilities) are counted. For example, if a school has only one teachers' room but it is in poor condition, then the school is not counted has having that facility. The basic statistics show clearly that most of the schools do not have the various types of rooms or other amenities identified, which is also why it would be so expensive to provide those facilities to all the schools. The exception is access to electricity, which is available in 92.0 percent of primary schools, and 86.2 of the primary schools that do not have an associated secondary school.

Finally, the last variables are indicators of unmet basic needs in the areas of housing quality, access to education, and the ability of households to make a livelihood. These indicators were estimated at the subdepartmental level with the 2002 census. In addition, a set of departmental geographic dummy variables is also included with the excluded reference category being Capital or Presidente Hayes depending on the regression (indicators of unmet basic needs were not available for Alto Paraguay, so the few schools in that department are not included).

Regression Estimates

Table 4.3 provides the regression estimates using standard linear regressions with robust standard errors. Four sets of variables appear to have a statistically significant

Table 4.3 Correlates of Primary Public School Passing Rates, Paraguay 2008

	All primary schools			Primary schools without a secondary school		
	Coefficient	t-stat		Coefficient	t-stat	
Urban area	−0.004	0.004		−0.011	0.007	
Combined with secondary school	0.000	0.003				
Classroom availability index						
CAI < 75	−0.047	0.006	***	−0.061	0.014	***
75 ≤ CAI < 100	−0.059	0.005	***	−0.074	0.010	***
100 ≤ CAI < 125	−0.052	0.005	***	−0.051	0.007	***
125 ≤ CAI < 150	−0.038	0.005	***	−0.037	0.008	***
150 ≤ CAI < 175	−0.029	0.005	***	−0.032	0.007	***
175 ≤ CAI < 200	−0.020	0.005	***	−0.022	0.007	***
Other school investments						
Direction room	−0.003	0.003		0.006	0.005	
Secretarial room	0.004	0.005		−0.009	0.011	
Library	0.000	0.004		0.000	0.008	
Laboratory	0.024	0.008	***	0.034	0.034	
Workshop room	0.014	0.010		0.041	0.027	
Multiuse room	−0.001	0.007		−0.005	0.015	
Teachers' room	0.004	0.006		−0.009	0.017	
Sanitation	0.046	0.032		0.030	0.036	
Electricity	0.016	0.008	*	0.012	0.009	
Piped water	0.000	0.003		0.000	0.005	
Computers	0.000	0.003		0.000	0.006	
Internet access	0.006	0.007		0.035	0.017	**
Unmet basic needs						
Unmet basic needs—housing quality	0.000	0.000		0.000	0.000	
Unmet basic needs—access to education	−0.001	0.000	***	−0.001	0.000	***
Unmet basic needs—livelihoods	0.000	0.000		0.000	0.001	
Department						
Alto Parana	0.040	0.011	***	0.095	0.034	***
Amambay	0.029	0.017	*	0.084	0.035	**
Caaguazu	0.036	0.011	***	0.084	0.033	***
Caazapa	0.013	0.013		0.067	0.033	**

table continues next page

Table 4.3 Correlates of Primary Public School Passing Rates, Paraguay 2008 *(continued)*

	All primary schools			Primary schools without a secondary school		
	Coefficient	t-stat		Coefficient	t-stat	
Canindeyu	0.040	0.014	***	0.094	0.034	***
Capital	—	—		0.022	0.042	
Central	0.025	0.010	**	0.068	0.035	*
Concepcion	0.044	0.012	***	0.097	0.033	***
Cordillera	0.059	0.012	***	0.098	0.034	***
Guaira	0.039	0.012	***	0.087	0.033	***
Itapua	0.021	0.012	*	0.081	0.033	**
Misiones	0.093	0.013	***	0.147	0.034	***
Paraguari	0.055	0.012	***	0.105	0.033	***
Presidente Hayes	−0.031	0.019		—	—	
Sanpedro	0.022	0.012	*	0.068	0.033	**
Neembucu	0.039	0.014	***	0.084	0.034	**
Constant	0.865	0.014	***	0.827	0.037	***

Source: Estimation using Paraguay 2008 school census.
Note: Statistical level of significance is 1 percent for ***, 5 percent for ** and 10 percent for *. — = not available.

impact on passing rates. First, there are statistically significant differences between departments in passing rates, as expected. Second, subdepartmental areas with high indices of unmet basic needs in terms of access to education have lower passing rates. Third, depending on the sample of schools used, the availability of a laboratory, electricity, or Internet access has a positive impact on passing rates. But the most important finding which is highly consistent in the two sets of regressions is the fact that the classroom availability index is a key driver of passing rates. Given that the estimation for schools with primary grades only is probably better (as mentioned earlier, when a primary school has an associated secondary school, it is not clear whether infrastructure inputs are used more at the primary or secondary level), we focus on those estimates.

In comparison to schools with a *CAI* value over 200, schools with a *CAI* below 75 or between 75 and 100 have a passing rate respectively 6.1 and 7.4 percentage points lower. After that, for values of the *CAI* between 100 and 200, the gains remain statistically significant but they are decreasing as the *CAI* increases. This suggests clear impact of the *CAI* on passing rates.

Should these results be trusted? As with any regression analysis based on limited data, there may be a bias in the estimates, whether this relates to omitted variable bias, sample selection, endogenous program placement, or measurement errors. But the results regarding the impact of the *CAI* tend to be fairly robust. Furthermore, it does make sense that a variable that directly affects students like the *CAI* would have more of an impact on the students than other variables that only indirectly benefit them, such as the availability of a direction room, a secretarial room, a workshop room, a multiuse room, or a teachers' room.

On the other hand, some of the omitted variables might lead to overestimating the impact of the *CAI* variable. For example, assume that a lower pupil–teacher ratio improves passing rates. The schools with a low pupil–teacher ratio are likely to have a high *CAI*, simply because many of those schools are small rural schools with few students and enough classrooms to accommodate them, given the attempt to have one classroom per grade in each school. To the extent that a lower pupil–teacher ratio is inversely correlated with the *CAI*, and that a low *CAI* is associated with lower passing rates, the omitted variable bias due to not observing pupil–teacher ratios could lead to overestimating the negative impact of low *CAI*s on passing rates.

This discussion hopefully clarifies that the estimations provided in table 4.3, while reasonable on face value, are not necessarily correct in that the interpretation of the effects is—as if often the case with regression analysis based on limited data—open to questions. But this is what can be done with the available data, and it does seem appropriate to inform policy with the (albeit limited) available evidence as opposed to using no evidence at all.

Conclusion

There is at least some degree of consensus in the education literature that better basic infrastructure in schools improves student learning. As a response, standards have been adopted in many countries as to what each and every school should have as a minimum. Such standards may be useful to promote necessary investments in schools. However, they will be useful only to the extent that they are realistic. In the case of Paraguay, the requirement that all primary and secondary schools be equipped with (among others) direction and secretarial rooms, as well as one classroom per grade, a room for recreation and physical education, a library, and a laboratory, is simply overly ambitious. The cost of providing these amenities would be simply too high, as discussed in chapter 3.

Rather than aiming to equip all schools with as many amenities as possible, a better approach is to try to assess which infrastructure investments are likely to have the largest impact on student performance. This has been the approach used in this chapter. On the basis of the estimation of an education production function, the evidence suggests that in Paraguay investments in classrooms in those schools that don't have enough classrooms are likely to bring larger gains than other investments. Furthermore, the largest gains tend to be observed when investing in the schools that are the most crowded in terms of lack of classrooms. These results were obtained with limited data and may suffer from bias, but they seem to be robust as well as intuitive, and thus provide a useful guide to policy makers for allocating scarce resources.

CHAPTER 5

Classroom Gaps and Targeting Performance of Investments

Abstract

Techniques for measuring school infrastructure gaps and the targeting performance of government investments do not appear to have been developed very much in the literature. Typically, studies only provide information on the share schools that lack specific amenities, whether this relates to classrooms or access to electricity. The objective of this chapter is to contribute to better measurement of school infrastructure gaps and the targeting performance of new infrastructure investments using techniques from the poverty literature. The illustration provided for classrooms in Paraguay suggests that needs are large, with most students being in schools that do not have enough classrooms. In addition, investments in new classroom construction made by the government do not seem to be targeted to the schools that need more classrooms the most. Finally, there may be some potential in using classrooms that are currently not in use in order to reduce the lack of enough classrooms faced by many schools.

Introduction

In many developing countries, the basic infrastructure of primary and secondary schools is poor. Too many students are crowded in small classrooms. Electricity, water, and sanitation may not be available. Amenities taken for granted in high-income countries such as libraries are not available either. In order to inform policy, it makes sense to measure school infrastructure needs and assess the degree to which government investments in new school infrastructure reach disadvantaged schools. And yet techniques for measuring infrastructure gaps and the targeting performance of government investments do not appear to have been developed much. Typically, studies only provide information on the share schools that lack basic amenities. In some cases, composite indices of infrastructure gaps combining different dimensions are constructed.

Much more could be done with the available data, and providing a richer analysis of school infrastructure gaps does matter because school infrastructure gaps as well as other school inputs affect student learning. A recent review by

Glewwe et al. (2013) of education production functions suggests that the availability of basic furniture (desks, tables, and chairs), electricity, school libraries, and high-quality walls, roofs, and floors all have positive impacts on learning. For Paraguay, this study has suggested that among different types of infrastructure investments, classrooms especially have the best potential to improve student performance.

The objective of this chapter is to contribute to better measuring school infrastructure gaps and the targeting performance of infrastructure investments using techniques from the poverty literature.[1] The idea of applying poverty measurement techniques to other areas is not new. These techniques have been applied among others to nutrition by Morris and Medina Banegas (1999), time use by Bardasi and Wodon (2010), carbon dioxide (CO_2) emissions by Makdissi and Wodon (2004), and child marriage by Nguyen and Wodon (2012), to name just a few examples. But to-date, these poverty measurement techniques do not seem to have been used for assessing school infrastructure gaps and the targeting performance of government investments in schools to reduce those gaps.

The specific focus in this chapter is on whether schools have enough classrooms to serve their student population and whether new classrooms are being built in the schools that need additional classrooms the most. The illustration of the approach is based on data from Paraguay. Previous studies on Paraguay have suggested that basic infrastructure is often lacking in schools and that budgets are insufficient to improve the situation (Brizuela 2008; Rivarola and Elías 2013). In comparison to other Latin American countries, Paraguay is one of the countries with the largest school infrastructure deficits (Duarte, Garguilo, and Moreno 2011; Murillo and Román 2011). There also appears to be a lack of formal rules in Paraguay for targeting new school investments. Allocations are dependent on requests from school principals and a possibly ad hoc assessment of whether those requests are justified (Brizuela 2008), which could lead to poor targeting of various investments in school infrastructure toward schools with the largest needs.

Using a school census implemented in Paraguay in 2008 with information on the number of classrooms available in each school, the schools' student population, and the number of additional classrooms in construction (as well as the classrooms not in use), this chapter provides estimates of what one might call, for lack of a better term, "school infrastructure poverty," and of whether new infrastructure (classrooms) are built in the schools that need those investments the most. The next section provides the methodology and a brief description of the data used for the analysis. The following section presents the empirical results. A brief conclusion follows.

Methodology and Data

A school is given a normalized infrastructure index value of 100 if it has all the infrastructure features it needs. This index can be related to infrastructure needs as a whole. In that case, some weighting scheme between the various types of infrastructure needs is needed (the weighting could be the cost of fulfilling each specific need). Alternatively, the index can refer only to a subset of the infrastructure needs, such as the classrooms available in a school for the illustration used in this chapter. Schools with an index below 100 are infrastructure poor, while schools with a higher index are not. Setting the "infrastructure poverty line" at 100, poverty measurement techniques can be applied not only to measure infrastructure gaps and identify the schools most in need but also to assess whether government interventions are well targeted.

Three school infrastructure poverty measures are used following standard practice: the headcount index, the poverty gap, and the squared poverty gap. In the poverty literature, the headcount index is the share of the population that is poor, that is, the proportion of the population whose consumption or income y per equivalent adult is less than the poverty line z. This would correspond here to the share of schools (taking into account student population weights) whose infrastructure index is below 100. The poverty gap represents the "depth" of poverty. This is defined as the mean distance separating the population from the poverty line divided by the poverty line, with the nonpoor being given a distance of zero. The poverty gap is a measure of the poverty deficit of the entire population, where the notion of "poverty deficit" captures the resources that would be needed to lift all the poor out of poverty through perfectly targeted cash transfers. In our case, a school with an infrastructure index of 70 will have an infrastructure gap of 0.3 = (100–70)/100, three times the value of the infrastructure gap for a school with an index of 90 (in equation 5.1., these gaps are normalized by the threshold z equal to 100). Finally, while the poverty gap takes into account the distance separating the poor from the poverty line (as well as the share of the poor in the population), the squared poverty gap takes the squared value of that distance into account. When using the squared poverty gap, the poverty gap is weighted by itself, so as to give more weight to the very poor. Said differently, the squared poverty gap takes into account the inequality among the poor, and this measure can also be used for infrastructure.

The headcount, infrastructure poverty gap, and squared infrastructure poverty gap correspond to the first three poverty measures of the so-called Foster-Greer-Thorbecke (1984) class of poverty measures. Denote by y_i the infrastructure index for school i, by z the school infrastructure poverty line (normalized to $z = 100$), by q the number of the schools lacking infrastructure (weighted by the student population), and by n the total number of school (again, weighted by the student population). The general formula for this class of measures depends on a parameter α, which takes a value of zero for the headcount, one for the infrastructure poverty gap, and two for the squared infrastructure poverty gap in the following expression:

$$P\alpha = \frac{1}{n}\sum_{i=1}^{q}\left[\frac{z-y_i}{z}\right]^{\alpha} \qquad (5.1)$$

It is important to use the school infrastructure poverty gap and the squared infrastructure poverty gap in addition to the headcount or incidence for evaluation purposes. Basing the evaluation of policies on the headcount index only may lead to favoring policies that lift schools that are just under the infrastructure norm above that threshold. By contrast, basing evaluations of policies on the infrastructure poverty gap or squared poverty gap puts more emphasis on helping schools that are further away from the infrastructure threshold and thus most in need.

For the illustration presented in this chapter, the variable of interest $y_i = CAI_i$ is the number of classrooms available in a school normalized by the number of classrooms that should be available so that a value of 100 means that the school has exactly the number of classrooms it needs, given its student population (all schools with an index value at or above 100 are not infrastructure poor). The database is a school census implemented in Paraguay in 2008, which includes (among others) information on the number of classrooms available in each school, the schools' student population (used as weight), the number of additional classrooms in construction, and the number of classrooms not in use. The infrastructure or more precisely classroom availability index CAI_i is defined as before as follows:

$$CAI_i = \frac{CU_i \times n \times 100}{P_i + S_i} \quad \text{with} \quad n = 20, 25, 30 \tag{5.2}$$

In equation (5.2), CU_i is the number of classrooms in use in a school and P_i and S_i are the number of students in primary and secondary schools, respectively (some schools combine both education cycles, but most do not). The variable n is a normative threshold that represents the number of students that should be associated with each classroom. Given that the standard classroom in Paraguay is supposed to be 7.2 meter by 7.2 meter, only a limited number of students will fit comfortably in any given classroom. Our baseline value is as before $n = 30$, which means that a school with 90 students should have three classrooms. If it has three classrooms, then the value of y_i will be 100, which is at the infrastructure poverty line. If it has less than three classrooms, the school will be infrastructure poor. For example, if it has two classrooms, or two thirds percent of its needs, the value of y_i will be 67. Due to lack of information in the database available to us on double shifts, the norm $n = 30$ may be too strict, but it may also not be ambitions enough. To test for the sensitivity of the results to the choice of alternative norms, we also use $n = 20$ and $n = 25$.

The baseline school infrastructure measures are based on the infrastructure index (2), but two additional indices are also estimated. First, when assessing the targeting performance of investments in infrastructure, we include in the infrastructure index not only the classrooms in use but also the classrooms under construction, so that $CAI_i = (CU_i+CC_i) \times n \times 100/(P_i+S_i)$ where CC_i is the number of classrooms in construction. Second, the database also includes information on classrooms not in use. When looking at how using the classrooms not in use in a school might reduce school infrastructure poverty, we also include those classrooms not in use, denoted by CNU_i, in the index, so that in that case $CAI_i = (CU_i+CC_i+CNU_i) \times n \times 100/(P_i+S_i)$. This gives at least some insights in terms of the potential impact on infrastructure poverty that using those classrooms would generate, even if this is probably optimistic, since when classrooms are not in use when a school does need classrooms, there must be a reason for this.

Two more caveats are in order. First, there is a requirement in Paraguay for all schools to have (at least) one classroom per grade. Many schools do not meet that requirement. But because information is not available in the database on the enrollment per grade, that additional condition for defining infrastructure poverty is not used (the ability of the schools to serve the student population for each specific grade is not estimated). Second, information is available in the database as to whether the existing classrooms are in very good, good, or poor condition. This information is not used here, even though one could have defined the school infrastructure index in such a way that classrooms in poor conditions are not included. This would only raise further the level of infrastructure poverty among the schools, but what is considered more immediately relevant is whether a classroom is used or not and not whether it is in good condition or not.

Beyond measures of school infrastructure poverty with and without the classrooms under construction (and in additional estimations with the classrooms not in use), measures of inequality (Gini index and general entropy inequality measures) between schools in the availability of classrooms are provided. Finally, a number of indicators are also provided for assessing the targeting performance of the classrooms being built, that is, whether classrooms are being built where they are needed the most. The targeting statistics are provided among schools that are infrastructure poor or not, and by quintile of infrastructure indices, with the bottom (top) quintiles representing the 20 percent of schools with the lowest (highest) infrastructure index.

The targeting statistics include (1) the average investment made in the schools as a whole, which, given the normalization of the school infrastructure poverty line, can be interpreted as the share of infrastructure needs accounted for by new classroom construction; (2) the average investments in new classrooms made among beneficiary schools only; (3) the coverage, which is the share of the schools that benefit from new classroom construction; (4) the distribution of beneficiary schools, that is the share of schools benefiting from new classrooms in various groups of schools; (5) the distribution of benefits, which represents the share of new classrooms being built by group; (6) the relative incidence of new classroom construction, namely the ratio of new classrooms to the existing classrooms; and finally (7) generosity, which is the mean new classrooms investments (normalized as a share of needs) received by all beneficiaries in a group as a share of the normalized existing classrooms among beneficiary schools in the group.

Results

Table 5.1 provides estimates of school infrastructure (in this case classroom) poverty in Paraguay for all primary and secondary schools combined with the baseline norm of 30 students per classroom ($n = 30$ in equation [5.2] from then methodological section). Currently, without the classrooms under construction, 57.9 percent of the students learn in schools that can be considered as being classroom or infrastructure poor in terms of the availability of classrooms versus the student population (FGT0 measure in table 5.1). Note that these statistics in schools are weighted by the schools' student population, which is why the analysis is described in terms of students and not schools. When the schools under construction are considered, the infrastructure poverty headcount drops to 56.4 percent, so that the classrooms under construction reduce the share of students studying in schools that are infrastructure poor by slightly more than one percentage point. The infrastructure poverty gap is at 19.8 percent without the classrooms in construction (FGT1 measure), which means that in all the schools slightly less than a fifth of the classroom needs are not satisfied. This drops from 19.8 percent to 18.8 percent with the classrooms in constructions. There is a similar decline in the squared infrastructure poverty index (FGT2 measure).

What is more interesting is to look at the targeting performance of classroom construction—are the classrooms being built where they are needed the most? In table 5.2, it can be seen that the average investment in classroom construction represents 2.6 percent of the overall needs of the schools. That is, assuming that as before an index of 100 implies that a school's classrooms needs are fulfilled, the magnitude of investment in new classrooms is 2.6 for the sample as a whole. For those schools where classrooms are actually being built, what is being build represents 21.2 percent of the needs. Coverage of new classrooms being built is relatively low, at 12.4 percent among schools that are infrastructure poor. This implies that most of the students who study in schools without enough classrooms do not have classrooms being built in their schools. In addition, coverage is about the same for students in schools that are infrastructure

Table 5.1 School Infrastructure Poverty and Inequality Measures ($n=30$)

	FGT0	FGT1	FGT2
Baseline without classrooms under construction	0.579	0.198	0.088
With classrooms under construction	0.564	0.188	0.082

Source: Calculations based on Paraguay 2008 school census.

Table 5.2 Analysis of the Targeting Performance of Classrooms in Construction (n=30)

	All	Poor	Non-poor
Average investment, all	2.6	1.3	4.4
Average investment, beneficiaries	21.2	10.2	35.8
Coverage	12.4	12.5	12.2
Distribution of beneficiaries	100.0	56.9	43.1
Distribution of benefits	100.0	27.2	72.8
Relative incidence	2.4	1.9	2.6
Generosity	19.2	15.0	21.5

Source: Calculations based on Paraguay 2008 school census.

poor and students in schools that are not. This suggests weak targeting. Indeed, while most (56.9 percent) of the schools (weighted by the number of students) where classrooms are being built are infrastructure poor, only slightly more than one fourth (27.2 percent) of the classrooms being built are actually built in schools (again, weighted by the number of students) that are infrastructure poor. Said differently, only a fourth of the classrooms being built are well targeted in the sense that they reach those students who study in schools that are infrastructure poor.

Clearly, new classrooms, which are identified in table 5.2 through the line "distribution of benefits" do not appear to be built where they are needed the most, with three fourth of the new classrooms going to schools that are not infrastructure poor. This is in part because classrooms are being built in rural schools to fulfill a mandate that all schools should have at least one classroom per grade.[2] Yet, this policy, while aspirational, does not seem to lead to building additional classrooms where they are needed the most. This in turn is detrimental, because as shown in previous chapters, investments in classrooms in schools that do not have enough classrooms bring larger gains than other types of infrastructure investments in Paraguay. Finally, the relative incidence of new classroom construction (ratio of new classrooms to existing classrooms) is estimated at 1.9 to 2.6 depending on the group, and generosity (mean new classrooms investments as a share of existing classrooms among beneficiary schools) is estimated at 15.0 percent to 21.5 percent depending on the groups.

A key question from a policy point of view is whether the assessment of targeting performance is significantly affected when the upper bound norm for the number of students per classroom is increased or decreased. It was mentioned earlier that the estimations of school infrastructure poverty are based on assumptions, and especially on a norm regarding the appropriate ratio of classrooms to students. The estimations in tables 5.1 and 5.2 are based on the norm $n = 30$, but it is straightforward to redo the estimations for different norms, and this was done for $n = 20$ and $n = 25$ in tables 5.3 and 5.4. Clearly, if more schools are considered infrastructure poor when the norm for classroom needs is more stringent (smaller value for n), it must be that a larger share of the classrooms under construction will be allocated to schools that are infrastructure poor. The question is whether this fundamentally affects the results.

As shown in table 5.3, with $n = 25$, 69.5 percent of the schools (weighted by the student population) are now considered as infrastructure poor, and the infrastructure poverty gap increases to 27.1 percent. The impact of the classrooms under construction on the poverty measures increases slightly, at 1.3 percentage point for the headcount. And as shown in table 5.4, the share of the benefits going to infrastructure-poor schools increases when the norm n is reduced, but note that even with a low $n = 20$, targeting performance remains very weak.

Still another way to show the results is to consider the benefit incidence analysis not in terms of schools that are infrastructure poor or not, but in terms of the quintiles of the CAI to which they belong, from the schools with the highest CAI to those with the lowest CAI. Note that changing the norm n does not change the quintile to which a school belongs—it simply shifts the CAI values up or down, but not the relative ranking of the schools in terms of their CAI. As shown in table 5.5, 48.5 percent of the new classrooms under construction go to the schools in the top quintile of the CAI—again suggesting very poor targeting by that measure.

Table 5.3 Sensitivity Analysis of Infrastructure Poverty Measures to the Norms Used

	$n = 25$			$n = 25$		
	FGT0	FGT1	FGT2	FGT0	FGT1	FGT2
Baseline without classrooms under construction	0.814	0.369	0.202	0.695	0.271	0.133
With classrooms under construction	0.803	0.358	0.193	0.682	0.261	0.126

Source: Calculations based on Paraguay 2008 school census.

Table 5.4 Sensitivity Analysis of Targeting Performance Indicators to the Norms Used

	$n = 20$			$n = 25$		
	All	Poor	Non-poor	All	Poor	Non-poor
Classrooms in construction						
Average investment, all	1.8	1.1	4.3	2.2	1.3	4.2
Average investment, beneficiaries	14.2	9.1	35.2	17.7	10.0	34.6
Coverage	12.4	12.4	12.1	12.4	12.5	12.1
Distribution of beneficiaries	100.0	80.7	19.3	100.0	68.8	31.2
Distribution of benefits	100.0	52.1	47.9	100.0	39.1	60.9
Relative incidence	2.4	2.1	2.9	2.4	2.0	2.7
Generosity	19.2	16.3	23.7	19.2	16.1	22.0

Source: Calculations based on Paraguay 2008 school census.

Table 5.5 Benefit Incidence Analysis of New Classrooms and Classrooms Not in Use

	Q1 (lowest CAI)	Q2 (second quintile)	Q3 (middle quintile)	Q4 (fourth quintile)	Q5 (highest CAI)
Average investment, all	0.6	0.7	1.4	1.8	4.2
Average investment, beneficiaries	4.7	6.3	10.1	15.2	34.3
Coverage	13.0	10.7	13.9	12.0	12.4
Distribution of beneficiaries	20.9	17.3	22.4	19.4	20.0
Distribution of benefits	7.0	7.7	16.0	20.8	48.5
Relative incidence	2.0	1.5	2.3	2.2	2.9
Generosity	14.8	14.0	16.5	18.3	23.4

Source: Calculations based on Paraguay 2008 school census.

Conclusion

Many schools in the developing world lack basic amenities. Measuring what could be referred to as school infrastructure poverty is useful not only to provide better measures of those infrastructure gaps but also to assess whether government investments in new school infrastructure are reaching the schools that need those investments the most. Using poverty measurement techniques, this chapter has provided a simple framework for conducting this type of analysis. The illustration provided in this chapter for classrooms in Paraguay suggests that needs are large with most of the student population being in schools that do not have enough classrooms. In addition, investments in new classroom construction made by the government do not seem to be targeted to the schools that need more classrooms the most. Finally, there may be some potential in using classrooms that are currently not in use in order to reduce the lack of enough classrooms currently faced by many schools.

Notes

1. For a general introduction to poverty measurement, see Coudouel, Hentschel, and Wodon (2002).
2. In Paraguay, the right to a free public basic education is enshrined in the National Constitution of 1992. The General Education Law of 1998 further states that the whole population should have equal access to education, and the article 141 of the law states that the Ministry of Education and Culture (MEC) must ensure that all schools meet minimum criteria in terms of infrastructure, pedagogy, administration, and financing. In its 1999 Decree 6589 and through Resolution 3985, MEC established standards for all schools providing basic education. According to those standards, all schools should have: (i) a direction room; (ii) a secretarial room; (iii) at least one classroom per grade with proper ventilation and light; (iv) separate bathrooms for boys and girls; (v) a proper space for recreation and physical education; (vi) drinking water; and (vii) a library. In addition, each school should also have a laboratory for physics, chemistry, and the natural sciences (Rivarola and Elias 2013). The provision of having at least one classroom per grade is likely to lead to the construction of classrooms in areas that may not need them that much.

Bibliography

Baker, B. 2012. *Revisiting that Age-Old Question: Does Money Matter In Education?* Washington, DC: The Albert Shanker Institute.

Bardasi, E., and Q. Wodon. 2010. "Working Long Hours and Having No Choice: Time Poverty in Guinea." *Feminist Economist* 16 (3): 45–78.

Brizuela, C. 2008. "Education Expenditures: Budget Tracking Analysis of Thirty Paraguayan Educational Institutions." Transparency and Accountability Project, Centro de Análisisy Difusión de la Economía Paraguaya, Asunción.

Card, D., and A. Krueger. 1992. "Does School Quality Matter? Returns to Education and the Characteristics of Schools in the United States." *Journal of Political Economy* 100 (1): 1–40.

Coleman, J. S., E. Q. Campbell, C. F. Hobson, J. McPartland, A. M. Mood, F. D. Weinfeld, and R. L. York. 1966. *Equality of Educational Opportunity*. Washington, DC: U.S. Office of Education.

Coudouel, A., J. Hentschel, and Q. Wodon. 2002. "Poverty Measurement and Analysis." In *A Sourcebook for Poverty Reduction Strategies*, Volume 1: *Core Techniques and Cross-Cutting Issues*, edited by J. Klugman, 29–69. Washington, DC: The World Bank.

Duarte, J., C. Gargiulo, and M. Moreno. 2011. "Infraestructura Escolar y Aprendizajes en la Educación Básica Latinoamericana: Un análisis a partir del SERCE." Nota Técnica, No. 277, División de Educación, Banco Interamericano de Desarrollo, Washington, DC.

Elías, R., M. Molinas, and P. Misiego. 2013. "El Desafio es la Equidad: Informe de Progreso Educativo Paraguay." PREAL and Instituto Desarrollo, Asunción, Paraguay.

Foster, J. E., J. Greer, and E. Thorbecke. 1984. "A Class of Decomposable Poverty Indices." *Econometrica* 52 (3): 761–66.

Glewwe, P. 2002. "Schools and Skills in Developing Countries: Education Policies and Socioeconomic Outcomes." *Journal of Economic Literature* 40 (2): 436–82.

Glewwe, P. W., E. A. Hanushek, S. D. Humpage, and R. Ravina. 2013. "School Resources and Educational Outcomes in Developing Countries: A Review of the Literature from 1990 to 2010." In *Education Policies in Developing Countries*, edited by P. W. Glewwe, 13–26. Chicago: University of Chicago Press.

Greenwald, R., L. Hedges, and R. Laine. 1996. "The Effect of School Resources on Student Achievement." *Review of Educational Research* 66 (3): 361–96.

Hanushek, E. A. 1986. "The Economics of Schooling: Production and Efficiency in Public Schools." *Journal of Economic Literature* 24 (3): 1141–77.

———. 1995. "Interpreting Recent Research on Schooling in Developing Countries." Working Paper No. 3, World Bank, Washington, DC.

———. 2002. "Evidence, Politics, and the Class Size Debate." In *The Class Size Debate*, edited by L. Mishel and R. Rothstein, 37–65. Washington, DC: Economic Policy Institute.

———. 2003. "The Failure of Input-based Schooling Policies." *The Economic Journal* 113 (485): 64–98.

———. 2010. "Education Production Functions: Developed Country Evidence." *International Encyclopedia of Education* 2: 407–11.

Hanushek, E. A., S. G. Rivkin, and L. L. Taylor. 1996. "Aggregation on the Estimated Effects of School Resources." *The Review of Economics and Statistics* 8 (4): 611–27.

Hanushek, E. A., and L. Woessmann. 2011. "The Economics of International Differences in Educational Achievement." In *Economics of Education*, Vol. 3, edited by E. A. Hanushek, S. Machin, and L. Woessmann. The Netherlands: North-Holland.

Hedges, L. V., and R. Greenwald. 1996. "Have Times Changed? The Relation between School Resources and Student Performance." In *Does Money Matter? The Effect of School Resources on Student Achievement and Adult Success*, edited by G. Burtless, 74–92. Washington, DC: Brookings.

Hedges, L. V., R. D. Laine, and R. Greenwald. 1994. "Does Money Matter? A Meta-Analysis of Studies of the Effects of Differential School Inputs on Students Outcomes." *Educational Researcher* 23 (3): 5–14.

Krueger, A. B. 2002. "Understanding the Magnitude and Effect of Class Size on Student Achievement." In *The Class Size Debate*, edited by L. Mishel and R. Rothstein, 7–33. Washington, DC: Economic Policy Institute.

Makdissi, P., and Q. Wodon. 2004. "Robust Comparisons of Natural Resource Depletion Indices." *Economics Bulletin* 9 (2): 1–9.

Ministerio de Educación y Cultura. 2008. *Microplanificación de la oferta educativa*. Asunción: MEC.

Morris, S. S., and J. M. Medina Banegas. 1999. "Desarrollo rural, Seguridad alimentaria del hogar y nutrición en el Oeste de Honduras." *Archivos Latinoamericanos De Nutrición* 49 (3): 244–52.

Murillo, F. J., and M. Roman. 2011. "School Infrastructure and Resources Do Matter: Analysis of the Incidence of School Resources on the Performance of Latin American Students." *School Effectiveness and School Improvement* 22 (1): 29–50.

Nguyen, M. C., and Q. Wodon. 2012. "Measuring Child Marriage." *Economics Bulletin* 32 (1): 398–411.

Otter, T., and C. Villalobos Barría. 2009. "Determinants of Student Achievements in the Primary Education of Paraguay." Ibero-America Institute for Economic Research Discussion Paper No. 198, Georg-August-Universität Göttingen, Goettingen, Germany.

Paxson, C., and N. Schady. 1999. Do School Facilities Matter? The Case of the Peruvian Social Fund (FONCODES)."Policy Research Working Paper 2229, Poverty Division, Poverty Reduction and Economic Management Network, World Bank, Washington, DC.

Rivarola, M., and R. Elías. 2013. *La falta de provisión de insumos escolares básicos en Paraguay: Identificando tamaño y las causas des problema*. Mimeo. Washington, DC: The World Bank.

Environmental Benefits Statement

The World Bank is committed to reducing its environmental footprint. In support of this commitment, the Publishing and Knowledge Division leverages electronic publishing options and print-on-demand technology, which is located in regional hubs worldwide. Together, these initiatives enable print runs to be lowered and shipping distances decreased, resulting in reduced paper consumption, chemical use, greenhouse gas emissions, and waste.

The Publishing and Knowledge Division follows the recommended standards for paper use set by the Green Press Initiative. Whenever possible, books are printed on 50 percent to 100 percent postconsumer recycled paper, and at least 50 percent of the fiber in our book paper is either unbleached or bleached using Totally Chlorine Free (TCF), Processed Chlorine Free (PCF), or Enhanced Elemental Chlorine Free (EECF) processes.

More information about the Bank's environmental philosophy can be found at http://crinfo.worldbank.org/wbcrinfo/node/4.

www.ingramcontent.com/pod-product-compliance
Lightning Source LLC
Chambersburg PA
CBHW081259170426
43198CB00017B/2848